GOD SHOWS NO PARTIALITY

THE FORGOTTEN SLOGAN OF THE EARLY CHURCH

DAVE BARNHART

ISBN: 1468110950
ISBN-13: 9781468110951

ACKNOWLEDGMENTS

Thanks to those from Trinity United Methodist Church in Birmingham, Alabama, who helped me workshop the chapters for this book: Leslie Bethea, Donna Burgess, Mike Burkett, Bruce Gilliland, Tom Himes, Celia Hutto, Amy Mezzell, Rich Myers, Amy Peake, Elizabeth Rogers, Pelham Rowan, Twink Scales, Butch Smith, Bob Trucks, Frank Vines, Lynn Williams, and Alys and Larry Wilson. Your participation in helping me discern the direction and structure of the book was a demonstration of how the Holy Spirit works through conversation within the Body of Christ. Your perspectives, comments, criticisms, and early edits were invaluable. Thanks to Lisa Elliott, Susan Bond, and Will Willimon for reading drafts of the manuscript and giving me encouragement. Thanks to designer Casey Patton, photographer Julie-Lynn Adams, and Norma and Dixon Aldridge for help with the cover art. Thanks most of all to Angela and Leo, who let me sequester myself long enough to get this burning thing out of my soul and onto paper.

CONTENTS

NOT A WEAPON

I looked up from my book and saw my five-year-old son squinting like a bombardier lining up his target, dangling the straps of his Bible carrying case between the bars of the jungle gym. A little girl below drew circles in the playground mulch, humming to herself. The bow on her head was at the center of his crosshairs.

I had let him bring his Bible to the park because he had taken to imitating me recently, hammering out "sermons" on an antique typewriter and carrying around a briefcase full of books. I was honored. When I had suggested an afternoon at the park, he had asked to take along his Bible—which he now dropped on the little girl's head.

The little girl wailed. Her mother and I both hurried over. She took the girl in her arms. "It's okay," the mother assured me. "It was only an accident."

"I wish it were an accident, but I saw him aim," I said. I picked up the Bible, dusted the mulch off of its cover, and ordered my son down from the jungle gym. He sidled up to me.

"What's the matter?" he asked.

Now he had my full attention, and I had his. I was a bit high on the symbolism of the moment. I could hear my voice in my own ears, intoning a Great Moral Lesson. "Son," I said, "the Bible is not a weapon. It is not meant for hurting people. If you cannot use it appropriately, I will not allow you to have it." I slipped his Bible into my bag and looked at him over the tops of my glasses. A point well-made, I thought to myself.

He stared at me. I could see his nimble brain working out a lesson of its own. Suddenly he twisted his face and began to cry. "You can't take God's word away from me!" he shouted. "That's my Bible! You are supposed to help people read the Bible, not take it away from them! What kind of preacher are you?"

All sounds of play in the park stopped. The birds stopped singing. Every child, every parent, and every squirrel in every tree turned to look at us. One empty swing creaked in the wind. My ears grew hot.

"That's it, chief," I said. "If you're going to throw a tantrum, we're leaving."

I marched toward the gate. My son followed behind, berating me the whole way. "I can't believe you would take away my Bible! What would God think of you?"

It was difficult to keep my composure. I tried not to smile. A ten-year-old boy held the gate for us as we walked by. My son was still shouting, "You wicked, wicked man! You can't keep me from learning about God!" I glanced at the ten-year-old. His mouth hung open and he stared, wide-eyed, at the wicked man walking by him. He had probably heard of persecuted Christians in other lands, but never thought he would see in his own neighborhood a father who wouldn't let his child have a Bible.

Perhaps my son and I both learned a lesson that day. I hope that he learned that the Bible is not a weapon. I learned that when you teach people that lesson, they sometimes get mad.

I have seen similar resistance from adults in college classes and church Bible studies. When I challenge literalist interpretations of the Bible with critical scholarship, when I question a biblical author's identity or theological reasoning, students may break down in tears or erupt in anger. They feel their Bible is being taken away from them. If people have used the Bible as a weapon to clobber gays, transgender persons, Muslims, atheists, feminists, and Christians who disagree with them, they are likely to react in fear and anger against attempts to disarm them of their favorite weapon.

My goal in writing this book is to give people the rhetorical tools to resist those who would use the Bible as a weapon. One of these tools is this slogan:

God shows no partiality.

This phrase was a defining idea in the early church. The slogan allowed new Christians from Gentile (non-Jewish) backgrounds to claim a place in the new Jesus movement. I believe today's church needs to reclaim this slogan from our past, and then proclaim it as a way to understand our inclusion of homosexual persons, our mandate to fight racism and privilege, and our distinctive witness in a religiously pluralistic world.

History versus Theology

Although this book is about "the early church," it is not a book about history. It is about who we as the church should be. In other words, the phrase "the early church" is *pre*scriptive, not *de*scriptive. Usually when contemporary Christians talk about "the early church," we're really talking about what our ideal church looks like, rather than about what actually happened in those first few chaotic days after people reported seeing Jesus alive. Historians tell us that there were many churches, many Jesus movements, and there were just as many diverse theological opinions in the first centuries about Jesus and the communities he inspired as there are today.

Yet church reformers are always trying to recapture the spirit of an ideal early church, to be more like the community that we think of when we hear the church described as the Body of Christ, the Blessed Community, or the kingdom of God incarnated in this world. Anyone who uses the phrase "the early church" has bought in, to some extent, to the idealized history told in Luke-Acts, where the believers "shared everything in common" and "were of one mind."

So have I. While I am skeptical of the *historical* truth of any church living together without conflict over beliefs, policies, or what color to paint the walls of their building, I do believe in its *theological* truth. There is a universal church, without denominational labels, which in spite of our differing opinions is somehow *one* in Jesus Christ. Wherever groups of Jesus-followers gather to worship and work toward the kingdom of God, and wherever they are open to the guidance of the Holy Spirit, the church is there. This same church has continuity with the church of the first century even though it has grown and adapted to carry out Jesus's ministry in this world at this time.

The vision of church I present here is just that: a vision. Yet I believe this vision is part of what has made the church compelling and effective in new times and places wherever it has taken root. This is the church that has proclaimed as its Lord a God who shows no partiality, whose grace always works around and in spite of human divisions, which always opposes the kingdoms of death with the Kingdom of Life.

Still, history informs theology, and vice versa. We can detect through the writings of the New Testament and from extra-biblical sources the tensions and theological dialogue of a church in search of its identity. Which leaders could speak for the new community? Who was in charge? Which teachings were authoritative? Who would be allowed at the table? It struggled with the implications of following a crucified-and-resurrected messiah. We still do.

It is with this sense of theology and mission informed by the history of the early church that I will begin many chapters with a story. I do not claim that these are histories or real events. Instead they are dramatic re-enactments of ideas and controversies. They function more like sermon illustrations than suggestions of what actually happened. My goal is to help clergy and laypeople get a sense of the urgency and vitality of the slogan "God shows no partiality."

In particular I want to avoid the suggestion that first-century Judaism and Christianity were monolithic or homogenous. Although I will sometimes talk about Jews and Gentiles as if they were clearly delineated groups, research over the last few decades has indicated that there was tremendous variety and overlap among people groups. It is partially because they were so diverse that the New Testament has such vitality. It was written as a way of corralling certain ideas into rhetorical family groups that later became doctrines, a task that must have been something like herding cats. We are inheritors of a rich theological dialogue from both Judaism and Christianity, and part of our task today is to figure out the trajectory of this millennia-long conversation about God. I believe an aspect of the conversation today's church desperately needs to hear is that our God is one who shows no partiality.

CHAPTER 1:

REGARDING THE FACE

God shows no partiality.
Romans 2:11

God's Impartiality

If you were to ask most contemporary Christians, "What verse best sums up the message of the early church?" they would have no problem telling you that it is John 3:16: "For God so loved the world that he gave his only begotten son."[1] But this verse wasn't written until more than seventy years after Jesus's crucifixion. For the church in the first few decades after Jesus's death, the answer would likely have been "God shows no partiality."

If the people of the early Jesus movement had driven cars, this would have been their bumper sticker. This sentence, or a variation of it, shows up in multiple books of the New Testament: Matthew, Mark, and Luke, in Romans, Galatians, Colossians, James, and the Acts of the Apostles. The best explanation for why so many authors in such diverse situations used a similar phrase is that it was a well-known saying and a commonly held conviction.

"God shows no partiality" is not the whole gospel, but it is an integral *part* of the gospel. For Paul, it was the reason Jews and Gentiles could gather at the same table, the reason women, men, slaves, and freemen could meet as equals, and the reason he felt he could preach with just as much authority as Peter or James. For James, it was the reason rich people should

---

1 The popularity of this verse has much more to do with football than with theology, and owes its popularity to "Rainbow Man" Rollen Stewart. See Chris Sprow, "Signing On: Sign Stories Are Long and Distinguished...and Sorta Scary," *ESPN*, September 3, 2008, http://sports.espn.go.com/espnmag/story?id=3566981.

show hospitality to poor people in Christian communities. For Peter, it was the reason he realized that he could associate with Gentiles, because God was doing something bigger than he could have imagined.

I believe it is a slogan that the church of all denominations and faith traditions should reclaim and proclaim. We should *re*claim it as a forgotten core value of the church. It reminds us of our history, of the struggle of the early church to define itself in the world of the first century. Then we should *pro*claim it as a principle today. In spite of all the ways we have of labeling and categorizing human beings as worthy and unworthy (male, female, or transgender; "native-born" American or immigrant; gay or straight), God shows no partiality—and neither should God's people.

I said that the principle of God's impartiality is not *the* gospel, but an integral part of it. I want to be very clear that I do not believe that all of Jesus's life, ministry, death, and resurrection were meant to proclaim contemporary ideas about inclusivity. But God's impartiality is an undeniable, inextricable quality of a gospel that is meant to be universal in scope. If the good news is that Jesus is Lord, then part of what makes it good news is that our Lord shows no partiality.

I also want to avoid the implication that this was a new idea. Divine impartiality had been part of Jewish theology for a long time.[2] But it was taken up with renewed vigor by early Christians who could see this impartial God working in and through Jesus. There were three ways that the phrase "God shows no partiality" functioned in the early church: as a slogan, a theological principle, and a core value.

Slogan, Theological Principle, and Core Value

It was first a slogan, not a doctrine. Slogans are about rhetoric. Doctrines are about theology and church life. Slogans are intended to inspire, incite, or infuriate. Doctrines are intended to clarify, define, and delineate. "What would Jesus do?" is a slogan, even though there may be some theology wrapped up in it. "We are justified by grace through faith" is doctrine.

---

2   For a thorough exploration of the roots of divine impartiality, see Jouette M. Bassler, *Divine Impartiality: Paul and a Theological Axiom*, Society of Biblical Literature Dissertation Series (Chico, CA: Scholars Press, 1982).

One of these you would find on a bumper sticker, the other in a creed or faith statement. Slogans work because they are versatile and can be applied in many different contexts. This is why when Paul is arguing that he has just as much right as anyone else to proclaim the gospel (especially those who were part of Jesus's "inner circle"), he says that though others might have been recognized leaders, "what they actually were means nothing to me—God shows no partiality" (Gal. 2:6). It's an off-hand comment. He makes a passing swipe at big-shot apostles by using a familiar phrase everyone knows.

Impartiality was also a theological principle. Paul uses it as part of an argument in what is possibly his most influential work, the letter to the Romans. Paul sets up his argument by lambasting pagan rulers like the emperors of Rome: "Claiming to be wise, they became fools; and they exchanged the glory of the immortal God for images resembling a mortal human being or birds or four-footed animals or reptiles" (Rom. 1:22–23). Suddenly his tone changes, and he addresses his Jewish and Gentile hearers. "Therefore *you* have no excuse," he says, "...for in passing judgment on another you condemn yourself." He goes on to explain that good is good, and evil is evil, regardless of who commits it, "for God shows no partiality" (Rom. 2:11). This slogan becomes the argument on which the whole opening of Romans hinges. His hearers are forced to look at themselves closely, erasing the distinction between "them" and "us." God judges our deeds, Paul claims, regardless of how we label and categorize each other.

In addition to a slogan and a theological principle, impartiality was also a core value of the early church. One way the early church demonstrated impartiality was by acknowledging women as leaders. Murals from third- and fourth-century catacombs clearly depict women officiating at the Lord's Supper or teaching as equals of Saint Paul.[3] We

---

3 Two that come to mind are the Eucharistic mural from the catacombs of Saint Peter and Saint Marcellinus in Rome (circa 300 CE) and the mural of Saint Paul and Saint Thecla in the Grotto of Saint Paul at Ephesus (circa 500 CE). John Dominic Crossan uses the latter as the cover for his book on early Christian origins and points out how these women have been silenced or relegated to the background. See John Dominic Crossan, *In Search of Paul: How Jesus's Apostle Opposed Rome's Empire with God's Kingdom* (San Francisco:

know from scriptural evidence that at least one woman, Junia, was considered an apostle (Rom. 16:7), and that women like Phoebe, Chloe, Priscilla, Mary, and Martha held important leadership positions in the early church.[4] These early communities depended on the patronage and leadership of women and met in women's houses, and it was likely the church's willingness to support women's leadership that helped the church grow so quickly in the first few centuries. Paul sums up the core value of impartiality in the life of the early church when he declares that in Christ there is no longer "Jew or Greek, slave or free, male and female" (Gal. 3:28).

Persons and Masks

The Greek word translated as partiality in Romans 2:11 is *prosopolepsia*. The stem of the word is *prosopon*, which means "face," "person," or "mask." Partiality is therefore literally "regarding the mask," and it makes more sense when you think about it in relation to the Greek theater. An actor (called *hupokrites*) wore a mask or "face" (*prosopon*) to change his appearance and amplify his voice. Just as villains in old cowboy movies wore black hats while the good guys wore white, the *hupokrites* would wear a mask that would easily identify his character: villain or hero, matriarch or beggar, god or beast. You could tell what role an actor played just by looking at his mask. *Hupokrites*, of course, is where we get our modern English word "hypocrite," but it did not originally have the same negative association we've given it.

That negative connotation comes from Jesus's own words. In Jesus's most famous speech, the Sermon on the Mount, he calls people who are obsessed with religious posturing *hupokritai*, hypocrites or stage actors:

HarperSanFrancisco, 2004). Recent research on women's role in the early church has inspired women in ministry, and archeology has filled in the gaps where texts have often been silenced. See Lynn H. Cohick, *Women in the World of the Earliest Christians: Illuminating Ancient Ways of Life* (Grand Rapids, MI: Baker Academic, 2009). and Sylvia Poggioli, "Pilgrims Trace Women's Role in Early Church," NPR, April 16, 2006, http://www.npr.org/templates/story/story.php?storyId=5342854.

4 See Eldon Jay Epp, *Junia, the First Woman Apostle* (Minneapolis, MN: Fortress, 2005) for more information about Junia.

So whenever you give alms, do not sound a trumpet before you, as the hypocrites do in the synagogues and in the streets, so that they may be praised by others. Truly I tell you, they have received their reward. But when you give alms, do not let your left hand know what your right hand is doing, so that your alms may be done in secret; and your Father who sees in secret will reward you. (Matt. 6:2–4)

Stage actors earn applause from people, not from God, he argues, when they draw attention to their alms-giving, their praying, and their fasting (Matt. 6:1–18). People can appear good and righteous to the public, but what is underneath the mask? Do not play with masks, Jesus tells his followers. Instead, do your alms-giving, praying, and fasting in secret. Jesus seems to echo the words of the ancient Hebrew prophets: Walk humbly with God, not ostentatiously (Mic. 6:8).

Human beings have a difficult time being impartial. Little things impress us: the way someone dresses, their pattern of speech, the kind of car they drive. We pick up subtle and not-so-subtle cues that tell us, "This person is valuable, hip, or interesting. This person is like me." Sociologists tell us that we all use "social discourses," ways of presenting ourselves to other people that identify what kind of person we are.[5] We advertise our social status, what groups we belong to, and our lifestyles all the time, even when we don't consciously do so. You can't opt out of social discourses. Even "normal" is a social discourse, and depends entirely on what you believe "normal" dresses, speaks, and acts like.

Social networking sites like Facebook and Twitter make social discourses even more obvious. People choose photos or avatars that present a certain image to the world. We choose a *prosopon* to project: flirty, adventurous, cool, or mysterious. We wear our favorite causes as badges, advertising to all our friends and family the kinds of people we have chosen to be. We wear a mask online and offline, and everyone—*everyone*—changes his mask to suit his situation.

There's nothing wrong with thinking about how we present ourselves. As I said, you can't opt out of social discourses, and even being "normal"

---

5 John Paul Gee, *An Introduction to Discourse Analysis*, (New York: Routledge, 1999).

is another way of participating. But we also use social discourses to judge others. We use racial profiling to figure out who looks like a criminal or a terrorist. We listen for catch phrases or linguistic clues to figure out where someone stands politically or theologically. We believe we know what makes a "real" man, or a "real" Christian, or a "real" person of value.

The God of the Bible, though, has a tendency to ignore our opinions of what makes a person valuable. God chooses an infertile elderly couple to be parents of a global family, a stuttering criminal to lead the Hebrews out of Egypt, and an immigrant woman as the grandmother of the greatest king of Israel.[6] Jesus and his contemporaries knew all of these stories, and they shaped the way they thought about their impartial God.

Two Sides to Every Story

The use of masks by actors suggests yet another nuance to *prosopolepsia*. Actors who wore masks would fulfill a certain role: villain or hero, comic relief or straight man. If God does not care about the roles, though, then all stories are subject to reinterpretation. Perhaps when the masks are removed, the villain and the hero, the fool and the sage will actually swap roles. If God does not regard the masks, then the story is wide open to interpretation.

One good example of an "unmasking" story is the drama of Tamar and her father-in-law, Judah, in Genesis 38. Tamar's husband dies unexpectedly, leaving her with neither a source of financial support nor a male heir. In the tradition of their culture, the responsibility for providing her with a male heir falls to her brothers-in-law. Unfortunately, the middle brother also dies when he tries to cheat her out of an heir.[7]

Judah grieves over his two lost sons. According to their tradition, the duty of providing Tamar with a child now falls to Judah's youngest son. Having already lost two sons to this woman under mysterious circumstances, Judah hems and haws about whether he will allow his youngest son to

---

6 The stories of Abraham and Sarah (Genesis 12), Moses (Exodus 4), and Ruth (Ruth 4).
7 God smites him for "spilling his seed on the ground." Apparently Onan believed he could cheat her out of her dead husband's wealth by not providing an heir (Genesis 38:8–10).

make love with Tamar. Years pass. Tamar is stuck at home, shamed and seemingly abandoned by God and her in-laws.

Tamar then comes up with a ploy worthy of classic theater. She learns that her father-in-law will be going on a business trip to the city of Timnah, so she disguises herself like a prostitute and seduces him while he's away from home. Like modern cheats, he may have believed that "what happens in Timnah, stays in Timnah."

After he has returned home and forgotten about the affair, he learns that Tamar is pregnant. Outraged that she has "played the whore," he commands that she be burned to death. Just as she is being dragged from her tent to her death, she produces evidence that he, Judah, is the father. Filled with shame, he admits "she is more righteous than me" (Gen. 38:26).

Like many great stories, Tamar's tale plays with the boundaries between right and wrong. On the surface, she is a wanton, a black widow, and Judah is the pillar of the community who speaks for society in sentencing her to death. But God shows no partiality, and knows that Judah is a hypocrite. God takes the side of Tamar, the woman seemingly trapped by circumstances beyond her control who uses her sexuality to win her freedom. Even situations that human beings consider scandalous violations of propriety, God may see as acts of justice.

The story itself unmasks something ugly about our society. Even today we use double standards when judging men's and women's sexual behavior, holding women to a higher standard while excusing men's bad behavior by saying, "Boys will be boys." Legislators and popular evangelists still loudly condemn what they perceive as sexual immorality even as they cheat on their spouses and sleep with prostitutes. This story in the first book of the Bible works as a subtle critique of anyone who would use the Bible to police others' sexual behavior. There is more to the story than the surface appearance of things, the author says.

In the New Testament, Matthew mentions Tamar as one of four women included in Jesus's genealogy (Matt. 1:3). All four women are involved in similarly scandalous stories, which indicate Matthew's awareness of a divine (and somewhat feminist) pattern in Jesus's ancestry. Jesus, like Tamar, will be judged by an unjust system and sentenced to death. Jesus, like Tamar, will be vindicated in a radical reversal that will unmask the earthly powers.

Think about what Jesus's death looks like from the outside: He is a would-be revolutionary messiah, hanging until dead upon a cross. His death may look like a scandal[8] or a failure to human beings, but to God it is both human and divine perfection, the ultimate expression of grace. Jesus's self-giving love, his obedience to the point of death, and his non-violent resistance to Rome and the religious leaders is exactly what God desires. Just as with Tamar, God sees beyond the *prosopon*, the mask, to see the real situation underneath. When Tamar reveals the truth and when Jesus returns alive, the powers and principalities that sentenced them to death are revealed as fakes and hypocrites.

For Christians, the scandal of the cross defines the way God operates in the world, a way that seems like foolishness to people who think themselves wise (1 Cor. 1:23). When Jesus says to the religious leaders of his day, "Prostitutes and tax collectors are going into the kingdom ahead of you!" (Matt. 21:31), he is expressing God's impartiality in the same stark terms that Judah uses when he declares Tamar's righteousness. Imagine the reaction he would get if Jesus told a group of self-righteous Christians, "Pornographers and drug dealers are going into the kingdom ahead of you!" Don't be fooled, Jesus says. God knows the score.

A Matter of Character

Divine impartiality was part of Jewish tradition from the beginning. Everyone knew that God was impartial when it came to judging someone's actions, and they expected judges and witnesses in court cases to be impartial as well:

> You shall not follow a majority in wrongdoing; when you bear witness, you shall not side with majority so as to pervert justice; nor shall you be partial to the poor in a lawsuit. ...You shall not pervert the justice due to your poor in their lawsuits. Keep far from

---

8 "Scandal" is a theological term. It often means a racy story in contemporary usage, but in the original Greek it meant a trap, a stumbling block, or a snare. A *skandalon* was something that offended people. Most modern Christians, lulled by hymns adoring Jesus on the cross, have lost any sense that Jesus's life and death were offensive or objectionable.

a false charge, and do not kill the innocent and those in the right, for I will not acquit the guilty. You shall take no bribe, for a bribe blinds the officials, and subverts the cause of those who are in the right. You shall not oppress a resident alien; you know the heart of an alien, for you were aliens in the land of Egypt. (Exod. 23:3–9)

The Hebrew Bible is full of passages that reject discriminating among people based on their wealth. Jesus's contemporaries knew that their God "shows no partiality to nobles, nor regards the rich more than the poor, for they are all the work of his hands" (Job 34:19). When King Jehosophat sent out judges to carry out his reforms in Judah, he told them to be sure that they judged fairly, because "there is no perversion of justice with YHWH our God, or partiality, or taking of bribes" (2 Chron. 19:7). When the powerful did pervert justice to take away property from the poor, God was livid. "It is you who have devoured the vineyard; the spoil of the poor is in your houses," Isaiah writes. "What do you mean by crushing my people, by grinding the face of the poor?" (Isa. 3:14-15). The rich who had used contract law and fine print to steal from the poor would then march into the temple and offer sacrifices to God, hiding their evil deeds with a religious facade. The prophet Amos lambastes these religious hypocrites:

I hate, I despise your festivals, and I take no delight in your solemn assemblies. Even though you offer me your burnt-offerings and grain-offerings, I will not accept them; and the offerings of well-being of your fatted animals I will not look upon. Take away from me the noise of your songs; I will not listen to the melody of your harps. But let justice roll down like waters, and righteousness like an ever-flowing stream. (Amos 5:21–24)

This kind of religious posturing on the part of elites would not fool God. Jesus ben Sirach, writing two hundred years before Jesus of Nazareth, advised religious people not to try to bribe God with sacrifices for their mistreatment of others because "the Lord is the judge, and with him there is no partiality" (Sir. 35:15).[9]

Biblical authors often point out that human beings are often poor judges of character. We get hung up on external markers of class and group identity. God, however, sees reality through the lens of love. God is not impressed with tailored suits and upper-class values. As James writes:

> My brothers and sisters, do you with your acts of favoritism really believe in our glorious Lord Jesus Christ? For if a person with gold rings and in fine clothes comes into your assembly, and if a poor person in dirty clothes also comes in, and if you take notice of the one wearing the fine clothes and say, "Have a seat here, please," while to the one who is poor you say, "Stand there," or, "Sit at my feet," have you not made distinctions among yourselves, and become judges with evil thoughts? (James 2:1–4)

The problem is most of us are not even aware of it when we show partiality. We are so used to the world of appearances, to the theater of everyday life, that we miss the real drama that God is enacting all around us. There are forces of evil in the world and in our own hearts that are heavily invested in maintaining the illusions that justify oppression. When Jesus began to unmask the prejudices and social sins of the powerful people around him, he made himself some bitter enemies.

Chosen and Unchosen

The theme of God's impartiality runs throughout the Bible, but it butts up against another theme: God's partiality in claiming a particular nation for God's own. What could be better evidence for God's partiality than the narrative of God choosing Israel as God's special people, and making a covenant with them? In liberating the Hebrew slaves of Egypt, God acts decisively to claim a particular nation for God's self. "You shall be holy

---

9 Sirach (or Ecclesiasticus) is one of the books of the Apocrypha, and is not found in Protestant Bibles.

to me," says God, "For I, YHWH, am holy, and I have separated you from the other peoples to be mine" (Lev. 20:26). Some biblical authors qualified this perspective with a measure of humility. They understood that the reason God had chosen Israel was not because they were especially good, but because other nations were "abominable" (Lev. 18:24). God gave the Israelites the Torah, the Law of Moses, so that they would not similarly become abominable and be "vomited out of the land" (Lev. 18:28 and Deut. 28).

Yet other biblical authors critique this usual understanding of being chosen and being unchosen, and the critique shows up in the first chapters of the Bible. It is the story of the murder of Abel by his brother Cain. Cain's motive is that he believes God is playing favorites (Genesis 4).

In this story, the two brothers both bring offerings to God. We don't know exactly what happens afterward. Maybe Abel's flock prospers, while Cain's wheat withers in the sun. We're told only that God pays attention to one brother's offering and not the other. When Cain complains, God actually sounds a bit defensive: "If you do well, will you not be raised up?" (Gen. 4:7). Any believer who is honest with himself about the way the world really works knows the right answer is "No." Plenty of people do all the good they can, only to see their efforts fail. Both Jesus and the author of Ecclesiastes know that the rain falls and the sun shines both on the good and the wicked, and all eventually die (Eccles. 9:1–6; Matt. 5:45).

Though this passage has been preached countless times from the countless pulpits, many preachers have come to God's defense, claiming that Cain must have done something wrong. It must be, they argue, that Cain's heart was not in the right place. But the text remains silent on the reason. What's more, if you look at the echoes of this story through the Bible, you see that family strife in the Bible almost always happens because someone plays favorites: Jacob and Esau struggle because their parents play favorites (Gen. 25:28); Rachel and Leah fight because their husband plays favorites (Gen. 29:30); Joseph's brothers sell him into slavery because his father plays favorites (Gen. 37:4). It seems that God establishes a trend that dominates families in the first book of the Bible. Maybe this is the root of sin: We all believe there's not enough of God's love to go around. Does God play favorites? Or is God impartial?

Some biblical authors felt that material prosperity was a sign of God's approval, and poverty and misfortune were a sign of God's disapproval. Bad things happen because people sin, and good things happen because people obey God: "The good leave an inheritance to their children's children, but the sinner's wealth is laid up for the righteous" (Prov. 13:22). There is, of course, some truth to this conventional wisdom. Hard work and right living often do pay off, and sometimes they are their own reward. Likewise there are negative consequences to misbehavior.

But this view of the world can quickly become justification for oppression, and can legitimize corrupt power. If the good prosper and the wicked do not, then the poor must be poor *because* they are wicked, and the wealthy must be wealthy *because* they are good. The modern version of this childish way of thinking is still very present in our political discourse. The twin clichés of the wealthy, industrious job-creator (who is likely a white male) and the lazy, addicted welfare queen (a black female) still dominate discussions of taxation and government policies. The author of Proverbs probably knew this, because the very next verse in Proverbs is, "The field of the poor may yield much food, but it is swept away through injustice" (13:23). This proverb indicates that material blessings are not necessarily a sign of God's partiality, and that poverty can be a result of oppression.

The author of the book of Job also struggles with how to make sense of fortune and God's favor. When God allows family tragedy, financial disaster, and chronic illness to afflict Job, his friends, playing the role of good, religious people, argue that we all deserve what happens to us, that everything happens for a reason, and that God is either punishing Job or trying to instruct him in some way. Job responds that if so, God is a lousy teacher:

Look, my eye has seen all this, my ear has heard and understood it. What you know, I also know…Will you speak falsely for God and speak deceitfully for him? Will you show partiality toward him? Will you plead the case for God? (Job 13:1, 7–8)

Job needles his friends for showing partiality toward God, as if God really were the defendant and they were the judges. If all of Job's suffering is punishment, he argues, then God, the judge, should give him his day in court (23:4–5). Elihu rebukes him, claiming that God is one who shows no partiality to nobles, nor regards the rich more than the poor, for they are all the work of his hands. (34:19)

This struggle with the partiality of God and what it meant to be chosen or unchosen was rooted in Israel's own experience. Even though the Israelites were God's chosen people, God's favor did not protect them from Babylon in 587 BCE. In that year the armies of the Empire of Babylon came crashing through the walls of Jerusalem and destroyed the temple, the very house of God. They led the residents of Jerusalem away in chains. Even though the survivors would be allowed to return home fifty years later, the Babylonian exile shook their understanding of what it meant to be God's chosen people.

> By the rivers of Babylon
> There we sat down and there we wept
> When we remembered Zion.
> …If I forget you, O Jerusalem,
> Let my right hand wither!
> Let my tongue cleave to the roof of my mouth
> If I do not remember you,
> If I do not set Jerusalem above my highest joy. (Psalm 137)

In the shadow of this destruction, the survivors asked, Why had God let this happen to us? "O God, why do you cast us off forever? Why does your anger smoke against the sheep of your pasture?" (Ps. 74:1). Biblical authors like the prophets put forward various theories as to why God had turned away from God's chosen people: perhaps they had violated God's conditional covenant in Deuteronomy. Perhaps they had worshiped idols. Perhaps they had been unjust to the poor. Perhaps they became morally lax. Therefore God punished them for their wrongs.

Yet not all the biblical authors were convinced of these explanations. After detailing all kinds of suffering, one psalmist says,

All this has come upon us, *yet we have not forgotten you or been false to your covenant.* Our heart has *not* turned back, nor have our steps departed from your way, yet you have broken us in the haunt of jackals and covered us with deep darkness. (Ps. 44:17– 19; italics added)

Aside from Job, there aren't many scriptures where this minority opinion gets expressed. But the nagging feeling that God has been unfair breaks through in some surprising places. Isaiah admits that perhaps devastation at the hands of the Babylonians may have been extreme: "Speak tenderly to Jerusalem, and cry to her that she has served her term, that her penalty is paid, that she has received from the Lord's hand *double* for all her sins" (Is. 40:1–2; italics added).

Their suffering at the hands of the Babylonians led them to reflect on what it means to be chosen, and to come up with some earth-shaking conclusions. Maybe being chosen wasn't about having the mightiest nation, the grandest temple, or an eternal monarchy. Maybe being chosen was about something else entirely.

Following this train of thought, Isaiah imagines what surrounding nations will say in their history books about the nation of Israel.

But he was wounded for our transgressions, crushed for our iniquities; upon him was the punishment that made us whole, and by his bruises are healed. (Isa. 53:5)

By a *perversion of justice* he was taken away. Who could have imagined his future? For he was cut off from the land of the living, stricken for the transgression of my people. (Isa. 53:8; italics added)

Holy and set-apart Israel is like a sacrificial lamb led to the slaughter, an offering to God that would reconcile other nations to God. Israel's faithfulness to God in exile would lead people to know YHWH as the one true God. Its restoration would create a new world order.

It's with this new vision that God says to the returning exiles:

It is too light a thing that you should be my servant to raise up the tribes of Jacob and to restore the survivors of Israel; I will give you as a light to the nations, that my salvation may reach to the end of the earth. (Isa. 49:6)

God's vision of Israel's chosen-ness goes global. Being chosen is no longer just about one ethnic group of people establishing a kingdom forever. It is now about changing the world.

I have given you as a covenant to the people, a light to the nations, to open the eyes that are blind, to bring out the prisoners from the dungeon, from the prison those who sit in darkness. (Isa. 42:6–7)

The whole point of choosing Israel, Isaiah asserts, was that God would include all of humanity in God's new kingdom.

And the *foreigners* who join themselves to the Lord, to minister to him, to love the name of the Lord, and to be his servants, all who keep the Sabbath, and do not profane it, and hold fast my covenant—these I will bring to my holy mountain, and make them joyful in my house of prayer; their burnt-offerings and their sacrifices will be accepted on my altar; for my house shall be called a house of prayer *for all peoples {nations}*. Thus says the Lord God, who gathers the outcasts of Israel, I will gather *others* to them besides those already gathered. (Isa. 56:6–8; italics added)

Isaiah's vision of a restored Jerusalem that is a house of prayer for all peoples, all ethnic groups, and all nations echoes the covenant God makes with Abraham over a thousand years earlier. God's original covenant was that God would bless Abraham and Sarah so that in them "all the families of the earth shall be blessed" (Gen. 12:3). God's choice is not for Abraham and Sarah alone, but for the world. If God shows partiality to one family or nation, it is only so that God can reveal God's impartiality in the end. The temple will no longer be for Israelites alone, but for all people to worship YHWH, the one true God.

God's Partiality

There will always be people who object to divine impartiality either on philosophical or historical grounds. Stanley Hauerwas argues that it is God's particularity, not God's impartiality, which best describes God's love:

> For God as the impartial lover is no more than the ultimate bureaucrat treating all persons and cases fairly. But we know that for all their fairness bureaucrats cannot help being unjust, as they are unable to see that the differences between us make it impossible to treat us all equally.[10]

I hope that reading Israel's history from the perspective of divine impartiality and understanding it as "unmasking" will help clarify what I mean when I say "God shows no partiality." When early Christians used the slogan, they were not describing a bureaucratic God who operates on a generic principle of equality or inclusivity. They were describing the radical action of a self-giving God in Jesus Christ, whose justice overcomes all human ways of labeling and categorizing others. This is a God who cannot be fooled by pretensions of religious behavior, or orthodox belief, or sacrificial bribery. When we describe God as impartial, we are describing what God is not: partial, as human beings are. It is a feature of God's ability to know the perfect truth about people and situations.

Ultimately, God's partiality is best expressed not in the concept of chosen-ness or election (whether those words indicate Israelites, Christians, or other "saved" people), but in God's particular interest in the powerless: "the widow, the orphan, and the alien." Miroslav Volf explains it this way:

---

10 Stanley Hauerwas, "The August Partiality of God's Love," *Reformed Journal* 39, no. 5 (1989), 11.

In the biblical traditions, when God looks at a widow…God does not see a "free and rational agent," but a woman with no standing in society. When God looks at a sojourner, God does not see simply a human being, but a stranger, cut off from the network of relations, subject to prejudice and scapegoating. How does the God who "executes justice for the oppressed" act toward widows and strangers? Just as God acts toward any other human being? No. God is partial to them.

Why is God partial to widows and strangers? In a sense, because God is partial to everyone—including the powerful, whom God resists in order to protect the widow and the stranger. God sees each human being concretely, the powerful no less than the powerless. God notes not only their common humanity, but also their specific histories, their particular psychological, social, and embodied selves with their particular needs.[11]

This is where the original sense of *prosopolepsia* makes more sense than our word, partiality. God sees beyond the mask or the obvious social situation.[12] God understands that the roles may be reversed when the masks are removed. For Philo, a Jewish philosopher who was a contemporary of Jesus, this best explained God's special concern for Israel. Philo said that Israel was like an orphan, an isolated nation that had no defenders.[13] God has a special concern for orphans and those who have no human advocates to take up their cause.

God's impartiality begins not with the assumption that "all persons are created equal," but with the assumption that pretensions of equality in an unjust world are simply one more mask. It is downright dishonest to say that class, or ethnicity, or gender, or sexual orientation do not matter in our

---

11   Miroslav Volf, *Exclusion and Embrace* (Nashville: Abingdon, 1996), 221–22.
12   For a good analysis of the problems with God's partiality and impartiality, see Stephen J. Pope, "Proper and Improper Partiality and the Preferential Option for the Poor," *Theological Studies* 54, no. 2 (1993).
13   Bassler, *Divine Impartiality: Paul and a Theological Axiom*, 91.

churches or our society. They matter a great deal. The flattening of all our hierarchies—wealth, gender, social status, nationality—presupposes a God who knows what the score is, and creates the possibility of a new community that intentionally rejects the old labels. God unmasks power and privilege and reverses roles so that the last are first, and the first are last. When Tamar is dragged before her father-in-law, it is she who is righteous and he who is not. When Moses stands before Pharaoh (who claimed to be divine), it is Moses who speaks for God and Pharaoh who does not. And when Jesus angers religious leaders by siding with sinners, outcasts, and foreigners, it is he who accurately reflects the activity of God, and the religious leaders who do not. God sees beyond the masks.

CHAPTER 2:

PORK, PRIDE, AND PREJUDICE

I truly understand that God shows no partiality, but in every nation anyone who fears him and does what is right is acceptable to him.
Peter in Acts 10:34–35

The Martyrs

An old man hung upon a wooden frame, arms and legs extended, a wrinkled banner against the sky. Beside him stood a soldier who wore an imperial uniform, humming tunelessly and tapping a cane whip against his thigh.

A younger man in fine clothes separated from the crowd of witnesses and ascended the raised platform. In his hands he held a bite of roasted meat, wrapped in a napkin. The soldier watched him bend close to the old man, but could not hear his words.

"For God's sake, Eleazar," said the young man. "It isn't even pork. It is beef. I promise. Just eat the meat. I will tell them that you have eaten swine flesh. Then we can all go home."

The old man sighed. He gave the young man a weary smile. "Look, boy. We have an audience. What would your friends say? That I'm old and weak? That at the end of my life, I turned against the God of my ancestors? What would I accomplish by it? I would live a week, maybe a month longer. And in order to have a few more days, I would lead young people astray. No, it isn't worth it. I still have to stand before the judge, our God, whether I die here or in my bed."

The young man straightened and stared at the old man. He shook his head. "Fine," he said at last. "It's your funeral." He dropped the napkin at the old man's feet, then turned and walked down the steps of the platform and through the crowd. The whipping began. The young man winced at the sound of human agony and hurried away.

The Judeans of Jesus's day knew this story by heart. It is found in the book of 2 Maccabees 6:18–31. Most Protestants are not familiar with it because it is part of the apocryphal writings of the Bible. It tells the story of devoted Jews who faced death rather than give up the markers of their religious heritage. Eleazar chose to die rather than to eat swine flesh, which his holy scripture called unclean. For some Jews of the homeland, retelling these stories would have fueled resentment toward their pagan Roman occupiers.

They told other stories of this kind of martyrdom. In one such tale, two women are humiliated and killed for following the ancient tradition of circumcising their infant sons. Soldiers force the young mothers to parade naked through the streets and finally throw them to their deaths from the city wall (2 Macc. 6:10). Still another story tells of a woman who watches as soldiers dismember and fry her seven sons to death, one after the other, because they refuse to eat swine flesh (2 Macc. 7:1–42). The story goes into gory detail, describing how even as the odor of her sons' searing flesh reaches her nostrils, she encourages them to remain faithful to the law of Moses.

All of these stories describe the brutality of emperor Antiochus IV. One and a half centuries before Christ (168 BCE), this tyrant began a campaign to wipe out Judaism from the land. He declared himself a god and demanded worship. His troops burned any Jewish religious books they found. He made it illegal to observe the Sabbath or any Jewish holidays. Instead, everyone was compelled by law to observe Greek holy days for Greek gods. Today we would call his policies "ethnic cleansing." His goal was to force everyone to assimilate or die.[14]

---

14 Some scholars have suggested that Antiochus has been unfairly represented in the Maccabeean story (see Jo Ann Scurlock, "One Hundred Sixty-Seven BCE: Hellenism or Reform?," *Journal for the Study of Judaism in the Persian, Hellenistic, and Roman Period* 31, no. 2 [2000]). Regardless, Jesus's contemporaries would have known these stories of past persecution and Zealots would have drawn inspiration from them. They would have fueled resentment of Hellenization ("Greekification") in the ancient world.

During the crisis, another author decided to write a book that would inspire his countrymen to resist assimilation. He would tell a story not about Jews resisting Greeks in his present day, but a time four hundred years earlier, when one exile from Jerusalem and his friends resisted the Babylonian empire. Today's Christian churchgoers know this story as "Daniel and the Lions' Den." It tells of how Daniel chose to be thrown to the lions rather than worship King Darius as a god (Daniel 6). God miraculously closed the mouths of the lions, so when the den was opened the next day Daniel emerged alive. His persecutors, though, were not so lucky. Darius had them thrown to the lions, and they were ripped to shreds.

Another story from the book of Daniel tells of Daniel's friends, Shadrach, Meshach, and Abednego (Daniel 3). Rather than worship the king, they chose to be thrown into a fiery furnace (much like the widow's seven sons). In the midst of the raging inferno, the guards could see a fourth figure walking around with the three friends. When they emerged, not even the stink of smoke clung to them. Like Eleazar and the widow's family, Daniel and his friends refused to eat pork or meat sacrificed to pagan gods (Dan. 1:8–17). They were completely committed to following the law God had given Moses, and would die rather than intentionally break it. Because of their faithfulness, God refused to let their enemies win. The message for Jews in 168 BCE was clear: Even in the midst of genocide, God would be with them. In life or in death, they could trust in God.

Christian Misunderstanding

Because today's Christians do not know this history, many of them continue to believe that the Pharisees of Jesus's day were legalistic and hypocritical for insisting on certain Jewish traditions, like eating only certain foods. American Christians, chowing down merrily on bacon double cheeseburgers, cannot see the religious importance of why eating pork matters, or why eating dairy with beef is a problem. For us, religious dietary laws simply make no sense. Unfortunately, this continued misunderstanding has also led to anti-Semitism and prejudice against modern Jews.

Being a non-Jew, I don't presume to understand food laws the way someone born and raised in a Jewish household would. But I do know that there are at least three things American Christians need to remember to appreciate any of the scriptures about food in the Bible.

First, it's important to remember that most of the world's religions have some kind of food regulations. Think about Hinduism (no beef), Islam (no pork), or even certain denominations of Christianity (no liquor). Even people who think they have no religious attitudes about food often make moral claims about food on cultural or nutritional grounds. If I were to ask most members of my church to eat horse or dog, they would object. "Horses and dogs are our friends!" they would say, even though people of other cultures enjoy these kinds of meat. There are nutritional taboos, too. We say that some delicious desserts are "sinful" and claim that some foods are good for us while others are "junk food." I'm not sure that an alien landing on planet Earth for the first time would be able to tell if these kinds of food regulations were "religious" or not.

Second, it's important to remember that the whole sacrificial system of Jerusalem was far more humane, dignified, and spiritual than our way of getting meat. I have often heard contemporary people—Christian, agnostic, and atheist—exclaim that the sacrificial system described in the Hebrew Bible was bloody, barbaric, and cruel. A simple comparison to our own practices puts this objection to rest. Imagine that you are a person in the ancient world of Jesus's day, or that you live somewhere in today's world where meat is rare. If you kill an animal for food, you thank God, the gods, or the animal's spirit. Because there is no refrigeration, any meat you kill must be eaten soon, so every time an animal is slaughtered you invite friends and neighbors to eat. Therefore you eat meat only on special occasions and only as a generous community event (i.e., weddings, holidays, and funeral gatherings). If you are an observant Jew of Jesus's day, you have your lamb slaughtered at the Temple for Passover. When you pray your prayer of thanks over your food, you intentionally remember the whole web of life that brings food to your table. By contrast, if you are an average American Christian, you pull up to a drive-through window and get your meat delivered to you in a paper wrapper. The burger you eat contains hundreds of ground-up cattle, which themselves were pumped full of antibiotics and fed grains their stomachs were not designed to digest. These terrified cattle were herded up a ramp and had their brains blown out with compressed air. No one thanked the cattle for their lives, or gave thanks to God for the cows. The sacrificial system, in contrast to our own way of getting meat, was part of a holistic understanding of the world in which life comes from God and life returns to God.

Third, food is part of our cultural and national identity. Food is seldom just something we put in our stomachs. We say that something is "as American as apple pie." When we go to baseball games, we expect to consume hot dogs, nachos, and beer, and when we stand and sing about popcorn and Cracker Jacks our eyes get a little misty. Americans "go out" for Mexican, Italian, Mediterranean, or Ethiopian food, and we talk about being part of a cultural "melting pot." People in churches share potluck dinners with nearly the same sense of community and tradition as the Lord's Supper in worship. Food is also political: When France criticized the United States' invasion of Iraq, the cafeteria for the House of Representatives renamed their French fries "freedom fries." Food is part of who we are. So when Christians read stories in the New Testament about Jews and Gentiles, we modern Gentiles have to remember that food and how we eat it is part of how we understand ourselves.

Jesus, his disciples, the Pharisees, and the crowds who listened to them argue had all grown up on the stories of Eleazar, the widow's son, and Daniel. For them it was part of their national identity, and they were far more conscious of this fact than people in the United States are about apple pie or freedom fries.

National Pride

The word usually translated as "nations" in the New Testament is *ethnoi*, which is where we get the word "ethnic." For the people of Jesus's day, there was no distinction between ethnic and national identity. The nation of Israel with its kings and borders had ceased to exist as a government hundreds of years before Jesus, but it still existed as an *ethnos*, a people and a nation. Diverse groups of people considered themselves "Israel," and they did not all get along. Josephus, an ancient historian, says that some of these groups were Pharisees, Sadducees, Essenes, and Zealots. Other groups shared roots in ancient Israel, like the Samaritans, who believed they were the authentic followers of Moses.[15]

But these Israelites increasingly felt like foreigners in their own land. Three hundred years before Jesus, Alexander the Great swept through the Mediterranean world and kingdoms fell before him, one after the other. Not only did he import Greek customs, clothing, and language everywhere he went, but he also left a cultural stew of East and West behind him. Alexander's mark remains to this day: Greek columns adorn buildings from Egypt to modern-day Iran. Murals from the first century in the places Jesus lived show people wearing Greek clothes reclining at Greek tables. Most big cities had a Greek theater and a Greek gymnasium. Even after the Romans took over, they continued to speak Greek and do things the Greek way all across the empire.

In these kinds of situations, minority cultures always face questions of assimilation and survival. In recent history, during waves of immigration to the United States from Mexico, Ireland, or Korea, some immigrant families faced questions like: What language will we speak at home? Will we let our children marry outside our ethnic group? What music are they listening to? What are these crazy clothes they are wearing? How will we teach them about their ancestry and their culture? It was the same in Jesus's day. Having survived the destruction of their capital city, exile to foreign lands, and occupation by a series of foreign armies, Jews still faced the cosmopolitan culture of the Greek and Roman world.

Some Jews assimilated while others resisted. Those who resisted used the same strategies that had helped them survive invasion and oppression in the past:

- They had their scriptures and historical writings (their past).
- They had the inspiration of martyrs and faith heroes (the present).
- They had hope in the coming kingdom of God (the future).

---

15   See Peter Miano, *The Word of God and the World of the Bible* (London: Melisende, 2001).

From their scriptures and stories of their past, they had the Exodus: God had freed their people from slavery in Egypt. God had struck down the first born of their Egyptian rulers. God had given them the law to order their society, and God had assured them that YHWH, this particular god, was their one and only God, and they would be God's chosen and set-apart people. God had gotten involved in their history to show that God was faithful, "slow to anger and abounding in steadfast love" (Exod. 34:6). God had defended them from the Philistines and from foreign armies that attempted to destroy the holy city of Jerusalem. After their exile, God had brought them back to their homeland. These lessons from the past gave them hope for the future: If God had delivered them in the past, God could do it again.

From the present, they had the inspiration of martyrs like Eleazar and the widow's family. These martyrs had remained faithful to God in the face of terrible punishments. Christians in the first and second centuries also shared stories of martyrs, telling stories of men and women who boldly walked into arenas to face lions or executioners. Even as they died, they sang hymns to God. Stories like these encouraged people to resist assimilation. God would deliver them either through miraculous intervention or through death and resurrection when God brought about a new kingdom on earth.

They also shared a hope for the future. Many Jews of Jesus's day believed that God would vindicate all those who had been unjustly martyred. They did not share the Greek belief of an afterlife, where souls were rewarded or punished in an underworld. Instead, they looked forward to a bodily resurrection in this world. When God finally established God's reign on earth, restoring the Temple and the holy city of Jerusalem to the glory of its golden age, all the dead would rise and be judged. With this hope in their hearts, they could face oppression—under Greece, or Rome, or any who dared resist God's coming kingdom.

This grand vision meant that those who believed in YHWH and followed God's commandments had pride in their nationality, their *ethnos*. They were God's chosen people. It must have been a glorious feeling. The only thing I can compare it to is the pride and love of country I feel watching fireworks explode above my city on Independence Day, looking at children's upturned faces brightened by the glare as they sing the words to the national anthem. But my country has only a centuries-long national history. Jesus and the disciples claimed a heritage that was over a thousand years old.

National Prejudice

There was a well-known saying related to an incident in Israel's past: "Cursed be the man who will rear pigs! And cursed be the man who will teach his son Greek!"[16] Folks who used such rhetoric were not merely content to believe that God had given them special rules as God's chosen people; other nations (especially those who ate swine and spoke Greek) were actually *inferior*. According to this view, any descendant of the nation of Israel who assimilated to the dominant culture was even worse than an outsider: He was a traitor.

I share this history to demonstrate that Pharisees were not simply being legalistic about food. They were trying their best to live according to the commands of God, scriptures that had kept their people alive and intact for centuries. It is important for Christians to have this background in mind when they approach the writings of the New Testament. Only then will they appreciate how radical and earth-shaking the idea of God's impartiality really is.

On one occasion Jesus tells his disciples that clean and unclean foods do not matter. In fact, he goes so far as to make a joke of it. All food, says Jesus, clean and unclean, goes into the stomach, through the intestines, and is turned into poop (Mark 7:18-19). Jesus himself never uses the word "poop," of course, but he's clearly aiming for scatological[17] humor: "Whatever goes into a person from outside cannot defile, since it enters, not the heart but the stomach, and goes out into the sewer." Whether you eat kosher or not, whether you eat a ritually clean roast lamb which was sacrificed in the Temple, or whether you eat something unclean like a pig or

---

16 Ernest Wiesenberg, "Related Prohibitions: Swine Breeding and the Study of Greek," *Hebrew Union College Annual* 27 (1956), 213.
17 "Dealing with excrement," i.e. "scat." Our English translations often lose some of the vulgar earthiness of biblical language and metaphor.

squid, all of the food you eat—clean and unclean—looks the same when it comes out of you. Jewish excrement is no cleaner than Gentile excrement. Therefore, Jesus argues, the food that goes into you cannot make you clean or unclean. Instead, the words and deeds that come out of you make you clean or unclean. Jesus parodies the religious concern over holy foods to emphasize his focus on ethics. Words and deeds have lasting value. Food does not, since it ultimately winds up in the sewer.

Christians who hear this scripture read from the pulpit seldom recognize how offensive it is. Think about this statement in light of the stories of Eleazar and the widow's son. Contrast Jesus's statement with the attitude of the author of Daniel, whose heroes would rather die than eat swine flesh. Jesus is turning the world of his listeners upside-down. Although contemporary Christians read Jesus's words and say, "Of course food doesn't matter!" some of his hearers would have been mortified. Imagine having grown up on stories of Eleazar or of the mother who watched her sons burn, only to hear Jesus's vulgar joke. "My ancestors died because they refused to eat unclean food!" people must have said. "How dare you suggest they died in vain!"

Certainly there were also open-minded Jews of Jesus's day who would not have been offended by Jesus's statement. Not everyone had confused national pride and prejudice with God's own attitudes. There were plenty of people with whom Jesus's message resonated, who believed in God's love of all of creation, and took to heart Isaiah's claims that one day, *every* ethnic group, every nation, would stream to Jerusalem to learn about Israel's God. But there were plenty of others who believed in their own ethnic superiority.

For these people Jesus's statement would have had the same emotional impact as telling a group of veterans that it doesn't really matter if people burn the American flag or not. I've received angry emails, forwarded hundreds of times, containing false stories of how some elected official or celebrity refused to wear a flag lapel pin or cover his heart during the Pledge of Allegiance, or act sufficiently patriotic. Usually these were not even real offenses, and most have been thoroughly debunked as urban legends. But what has never failed to impress me is the sheer force of anger, of vitriolic hatred toward someone who failed to respect certain symbols of national pride and identity.

Jesus's statement is a shot across the bow of national identity. Although it's doubtful that Jesus ever ate unclean foods himself, his statement that dietary restrictions don't make one clean or unclean erases an important distinction between Jews and Gentiles. He has blurred the boundary between chosen and unchosen. All are equally capable of being clean or unclean to God. Imagine the outrage, the howls of protest. If you can envision the kind of ire this would stir up, then you begin to understand why some people wanted to kill Jesus.

People who heard Jesus's statement that food cannot make you clean or unclean probably thought he was abolishing the law, that he was spouting dangerous heresy. He and his followers had to defend themselves against allegations that they were promoting an "anything goes" religion. "Do not think that I have come to abolish the Law or the prophets," he says. "I have come not to abolish, but to fulfill" (Matt. 5:17).

Today's American version of evangelical Christianity struggles with the same kind of national prejudice Jesus faced. For some Christians, their identity as "saved" depends on others being "unsaved." Some pastors have even claimed that God will not hear the prayers of Jews or Muslims.[18] One popular preacher and author claims that though Christians often say to "hate the sin but love the sinner," God actually hates sinners.[19] In our version of national prejudice, non-Christians of any kind do not have a place in God's plan of salvation or the redemption of the world.

By contrast, some modern Jews I know espouse a philosophy and an understanding of God that I think is probably closer to Jesus's own. I interviewed a local rabbi, Jonathan Miller, and asked him what he wished Christians knew about Judaism. He wanted Christians to know that Judaism was not a proselytizing religion because "other people already have a relationship with God," he said. "We just have a Jewish relationship with God."

---

18   Brian Kaylor, "Anniversary of Bailey Smith's Harmful Moment in Baptist-Jewish Relations," *Ethics Daily*, August 23, 2010, http://www.ethicsdaily.com/anniversary-of-bailey-smiths-harmful-moment-in-baptist-jewish-relations-cms-16564.
19   Greg Garrison, "Giving It Away: Brook Hills Pastor Pens Book Telling Christians to Avoid Worldly Wealth," *The Birmingham News*, June 12, 2010.

The Story of Peter and Cornelius

We've seen how Jesus's words about clean and unclean foods challenged the religious system of his culture. Keeping this background in mind, listen to this story of the early church from Acts 10.

> In Caesarea there was a man named Cornelius, a centurion of the Italian Cohort, as it was called. He was a devout man who feared God with all his household; he gave alms generously to the people and prayed constantly to God.

This story's action begins not with Peter or a representative of the church, but with a Roman centurion, Cornelius. Luke tells us that Cornelius is a devout, God-fearing man, but he is still a Roman military officer. To many homeland Jews of Peter's day, he is the enemy. He represents the government power that crucified Jesus. In fact, as a centurion, he may oversee crucifixions himself.

Recent research by John Dominic Crossan has indicated that Cornelius's devotion to the God of Israel may not have been that uncommon. In fact, there is archeological evidence that non-Jewish "god-fearers" may have played an important role in Jewish society all over the Mediterranean world. They helped finance the building of synagogues, studied the Torah, and served as advocates in Roman culture for Jewish interests. They may have been receptive to a message about a Jewish messiah who had extended salvation to Gentile believers.[20] Cornelius, his household, and some of his soldiers may have been some of these people.

This God-fearing Cornelius prays and gives alms to the people. He lives a righteous life, so God chooses to send him a message:

> One afternoon at about three o'clock he had a vision in which he clearly saw an angel of God coming in and saying to him, "Cornelius." He stared at him in terror and said, "What is it, Lord?" He answered, "Your prayers and your alms have ascended as a memorial

---

20 Crossan, *In Search of Paul.*

before God. Now send men to Joppa for a certain Simon who is called Peter; he is lodging with Simon, a tanner, whose house is by the seaside." When the angel who spoke to him had left, he called two of his slaves and a devout soldier from the ranks of those who served him, and after telling them everything, he sent them to Joppa.

In spite of his status as a Gentile and a Roman, God sends an angel to visit him. The author of Acts wants to emphasize that this is scandalous! For most American Christians it might be like hearing that God had appeared to a Muslim colonel in the Iranian army.

The next scene shifts to Peter. Luke takes pains to remind us of Peter's background. He is an exemplary first-century Jew. He does not eat unclean foods and does not associate with unclean people. Like most people, from the time he could talk he has known the difference between "us" and "them."

About noon the next day, as they were on their journey and approaching the city, Peter went up on the roof to pray. He became hungry and wanted something to eat; and while it was being prepared, he fell into a trance. He saw the heavens opened and something like a large sheet coming down, being lowered to the ground by its four corners. In it were all kinds of four-footed creatures and reptiles and birds of the air. Then he heard a voice saying, "Get up, Peter; kill and eat." But Peter said, "By no means, Lord; for I have never eaten anything that is profane or unclean." The voice said to him again, a second time, "What God has made clean, you must not call profane." This happened three times, and the thing was suddenly taken up to heaven.

Peter meditates on the roof while waiting for his lunch. While he is delirious with hunger, God shows him all kinds of animals that he would never eat because they were unclean according to the Torah: geckos and mealworms, pigs and camels, lobster and squid. When Peter objects, God tells him, "Don't call unclean what God has called clean."

Now while Peter was greatly puzzled about what to make of the vision that he had seen, suddenly the men sent by Cornelius appeared. They were asking for Simon's house and were standing by the gate. They called out to ask whether Simon, who was called Peter, was staying there. While Peter was still thinking about the vision, the Spirit said to him, "Look, three men are searching for you. Now get up, go down, and go with them without hesitation; for I have sent them." So Peter went down to the men and said, "I am the one you are looking for; what is the reason for your coming?" They answered, "Cornelius, a centurion, an upright and God-fearing man, who is well spoken of by the whole Jewish nation, was directed by a holy angel to send for you to come to his house and to hear what you have to say." So Peter invited them in and gave them lodging.

The next day he got up and went with them, and some of the believers from Joppa accompanied him. The following day they came to Caesarea. Cornelius was expecting them and had called together his relatives and close friends. On Peter's arrival Cornelius met him, and falling at his feet, worshipped him. But Peter made him get up, saying, "Stand up; I am only a mortal." And as he talked with him, he went in and found that many had assembled; and he said to them, "You yourselves know that it is unlawful for a Jew to associate with or to visit a Gentile; but God has shown me that I should not call anyone profane or unclean. So when I was sent for, I came without objection. Now may I ask why you sent for me?"

When Peter says, "You yourselves know that it is unlawful for a Jew to associate with or to visit a Gentile," it is probable that we are hearing the author's voice here, not Peter's, and the author is exaggerating. It is not exactly true that it was unlawful for Jews to "visit or associate with" Gentiles. In fact, the Torah makes explicit that foreigners in Israel were to be loved as neighbors (compare Lev. 19:18, 19:34). There were plenty of Judeans who associated with Gentiles, who traded and intermarried with them. The author even points out that Cornelius is "well spoken of by the whole Jewish nation." Peter's words are meant to display a religious attitude, though, that the readers of Acts would recognize as being common to zealots of the day. There were some "zealous" homeland Jews who did hold this extremist view, who believed that Greek-speakers and Gentiles were a stain upon the land.

What Peter says next shows that he already knows that there is a greater significance to his vision than God giving him permission to eat bacon. "God has shown me that I should not call anyone unclean." This also is not exactly true. God shows Peter that *food* is not unclean. But Peter knows that visions have deeper meanings. God is not merely telling Peter that pigs and squid are okay to eat. God is making the point that all creation, and all human beings in all their diverse splendor, are acceptable to God.

Cornelius next explains what God has shown him. Peter and Cornelius have both been summoned to this moment by God, and both will be changed by the event. Cornelius concludes:

> "Therefore I sent for you immediately, and you have been kind enough to come. So now all of us are here in the presence of God to listen to all that the Lord has commanded you to say." Then Peter began to speak to them: "I truly understand that God shows no partiality, but in every nation anyone who fears him and does what is right is acceptable to him."

Here Peter speaks some of the most gracious words uttered in the New Testament: "Now I truly understand that God shows no partiality, but in every nation anyone who fears him and does what is right is acceptable to him." Listen to this carefully: "God shows no partiality, but in *every nation* [ethnic group], *anyone* who fears him and does what is right is acceptable to him." Every nation. Among all the *ethnoi*, the nations, with all their diverse cultures, their food rituals, their religious backgrounds, *anyone* who follows God and does what is right is acceptable to him. Peter recognizes that he cannot regard Cornelius as an outsider any longer, but a fellow

God-follower whom Christ has also saved. All that remains is for Peter to share the story and message of Jesus with him:

> "You know the message he sent to the people of Israel, preaching peace by Jesus Christ—he is Lord of all. That message spread throughout Judea, beginning in Galilee after the baptism that John announced: how God anointed Jesus of Nazareth with the Holy Spirit and with power; how he went about doing good and healing all who were oppressed by the devil, for God was with him. We are witnesses to all that he did both in Judea and in Jerusalem. They put him to death by hanging him on a tree; but God raised him on the third day and allowed him to appear, not to all the people but to us who were chosen by God as witnesses, and who ate and drank with him after he rose from the dead. He commanded us to preach to the people and to testify that he is the one ordained by God as judge of the living and the dead. All the prophets testify about him that everyone who believes in him receives forgiveness of sins through his name." While Peter was still speaking, the Holy Spirit fell upon all who heard the word. The circumcised believers who had come with Peter were astounded that the gift of the Holy Spirit had been poured out even on the Gentiles, for they heard them speaking in tongues and extolling God. Then Peter said, "Can anyone withhold the water for baptizing these people who have received the Holy Spirit just as we have?" So he ordered them to be baptized in the name of Jesus Christ. Then they invited him to stay for several days.

In another demonstration of impartiality, the Gentiles receive the Holy Spirit before Peter is finished speaking. They don't do *anything* to receive this gift of the Holy Spirit. It simply happens to them when they hear the story of Jesus and understand what it means. Peter realizes he cannot withhold baptism from these people if God has not withheld the gift of the Holy Spirit from them. Peter follows where God is leading: toward full inclusion of Gentiles not merely as second-class "God-fearers" on the margins of the community, but as equal brothers and sisters. "Prior to meeting Cornelius," says Susan Bond, "Peter is captive to the assumption that confessing Jesus Christ creates a new community of insiders and outsiders, suspiciously like contemporary Christian 'superiority.'"[21]

I preached on this scripture on the very weekend that protesters marched in New York as they shouted in anger about a Muslim community center being built near Ground Zero. How would those angry people have responded if Peter preached "God shows no partiality" to them? A short time later, a fringe church in Florida planned a Koran-burning on the anniversary of the September 11 World Trade Center attacks. Had its members ever read these words of Peter's? These are words that should be printed on bumper stickers, plastered on T-shirts, and written on billboards. They are scandalous words that strike to the heart of Christian prejudice and exclusivism. God shows no partiality! The gospel of Jesus Christ is always breaking through the walls we build between us and them, between our culture and theirs, even between our religion and theirs. Peter, who two days ago wouldn't have dared rub shoulders with a Gentile, now stands in front of a Gentile Roman army officer, looks him in the eye, and says, "God shows no partiality between me and you."

The story of Peter and Cornelius in Acts is the story the early church told about itself. The author uses this event as a second Pentecost, a turning point in development of the early church. Although all of the first followers of Jesus were Jewish, and although the early church had a decidedly Jewish character, from this point forward membership would be open to non-Jews. After these events (according to Luke's story), Peter returns to the church in Jerusalem and meets with the church leadership. They resolve that Jewish Christians and non-Jewish Christians are now part of the same community, the Body of Christ (Acts 11:1–18).

Though the book of Acts makes it sound relatively simple, the matter would not be settled for decades after this encounter. Some Jewish Christians continued to insist that for people to be really Christian, they needed to follow dietary laws and be circumcised (Acts 15:5). Paul would continue

---

21 L. Susan Bond, "Acts 10:34–43," *Interpretation* 56, no. 1 (2002), 82.

to struggle for years with the tendency of some Christians to focus on the importance of food regulations and circumcision.

Today some Christian groups continue to try to form a "Christian culture" or fight a culture war based on food or clothing or rituals that show our superior dedication and loyalty to God. Christians have insisted, at various times and in various places, that good Christians should not dance, or swim in public pools, or drink alcohol, or eat meat on certain days, or study evolution, or read fantasy fiction, or marry across racial lines. Other Christians have resisted these kinds of regulations. We often struggle with the same things that the early church debated.

Food Sacrificed to Idols

When we talk about the food issue for the early church, it may help to think about it in three different time periods. First, there was Jesus's own ministry, when he walked about and taught his disciples. Second, there was the chaotic formation of the early church in diverse locations, from which we receive Paul's letters. Finally, there was the writing of the gospels. So although Jesus sounds almost nonchalant about food regulations in Mark's gospel when he implies that food cannot make you clean or unclean (time period three), it's important to remember that the gospels were written *after* many of these arguments had already been settled during the growth of the church (time period two). Instead of being a verbatim transcript of Jesus's own statement from time period one, Mark 7:18–19 may reflect the attitudes of the church after Jesus, or what they inferred from his teaching.[22] If Jesus really had spoken so definitively about food, it does not seem that it would have been a problem for Paul's churches, or for Peter and Cornelius. Indeed, the food problem clearly persisted well after Jesus's ministry, because the issue confronted the Corinthian church. The freedom that came along with the principle of God's impartiality created conflict in the community over whether or not to eat food sacrificed to idols.

Most of the meat available in city markets was from animals sacrificed to pagan gods at pagan temples. If a Christian convert was going to continue

---

22 It is possible, of course, that Jesus did say these words and their full import was not realized until much later.

associating with pagans, going to dinners, celebrations, and so on, he would almost certainly be in positions in which he would have meat sacrificed to idols served to him. So should he eat and possibly offend God, or not eat and possibly offend his host? Paul found himself having to tip-toe through this social and political minefield.

"Liberal" Christians didn't see a problem with eating meat sacrificed to idols. They knew that pagan gods did not exist, and they felt they could eat with a clear conscience. "Conservative" Christians were afraid that eating the meat would be spiritually dangerous. The controversy that erupted was not unlike contemporary religious arguments over alcohol or hip-hop or Harry Potter. Apparently there have always been Christians who feel that there is no harm in the things we consume and Christians who believe such things are dangerous.

But rather than just declaring one party right and the other party wrong, Paul tries to be diplomatic. It is not enough to be right on this issue, Paul says. You must also be considerate of your fellow believers, whether they are on the liberal or conservative side. To that end, he lays out a couple of different scenarios:

> "Food will not bring us close to God." We are no worse off if we do not eat, and no better off if we do. But take care that this liberty of yours does not somehow become a stumbling-block to the weak. For if others see you, who possess knowledge, eating in the temple of an idol, might they not, since their conscience is weak, be encouraged to the point of eating food sacrificed to idols? So by your knowledge those weak believers for whom Christ died are destroyed. But when you thus sin against members of your family, and wound their conscience when it is weak, you sin against Christ. Therefore, if food is a cause of their falling, I will never eat meat, so that I may not cause one of them to fall. (1 Cor. 8:8–13)

In this first scenario, Paul says that weak believers may be convinced to do something they *think* is wrong because of peer pressure. If they think they are doing something wrong, it wounds their consciences. Even if it is not a sin, it feels like it is! Putting people in such a position, Paul argues, *is* sinful.

> If an unbeliever invites you to a meal and you are disposed to go, eat whatever is set before you without raising any question on the ground of conscience. But if [a believer] says to you, "This has been offered in sacrifice," then do not eat it, out of consideration for the one who informed you, and for the sake of conscience—I mean the other's conscience, not your own. For why should my liberty be subject to the judgment of someone else's conscience? If I partake with thankfulness, why should I be denounced because of that for which I give thanks? (1 Cor. 10:27–30)

Paul lays out both of these scenarios in order to show that this is not just an "either/or" issue. It is about how believers show love toward one another. "You may indeed have the theological high ground," Paul says to the liberal Christians, "but are you being considerate?" Paul essentially argues both points of view in order to get the disagreeing groups to live in harmony. "Eat whatever you buy in the market with a clear conscience," he says in verse twenty-five, but don't do it in public if you'll offend other Christians.[23] The focus, he says, should be on Jesus Christ and whatever advances his cause: "So, whether you eat or drink, or whatever you do, do everything for the glory of God. Give no offense to Jews or to Greeks or to the church of God, just as I try to please everyone in everything I do, not seeking my own advantage, but that of many, so that they may be saved" (1 Cor. 10:31–33).

As someone who has had to mediate church disputes, I sympathize with Paul's argument, but I'm not convinced by it. Christians have often allowed terrible injustices to go on for the sake of maintaining harmony in their churches. They have allowed other Christians, in the name of Jesus, to trample on the civil rights of others. Churches have shown partiality against outsiders and reacted with fear toward all kinds of imaginary vices.

---

23 Paul's reasoning reminds me of a joke: Q: When you take your teetotaler friend fishing, how do you keep him from drinking your beer? A: Take two teetotalers.

I remember being told that playing *Dungeons & Dragons* with my friends would lead to demon-worship. I cannot deny that some sensitive young Christians may have felt dirty or scandalous rolling twelve-sided dice, as though they were flirting with the powers of evil. But when modern Christians with weak theology condemn kids for reading about wizards like Harry Potter, I believe we are dealing with a particularly nasty kind of partiality. It is the kind of social system that creates moral panics in order to establish social boundaries and determine who is a "real" Christian and who is not.

I suspect that the people who stir up such moral panics do so less to protect weak individuals and more to protect their own power. The president of the National Association of Evangelicals, Ted Haggard, loudly condemned homosexuality until the day he was outed as someone who slept with men and took methamphetamines. Osama bin Laden condemned the decadent West even while consuming its pornography. I resist the idea that these are the kinds of religious people whose consciences I should avoid damaging by dancing, listening to rap music, or reading stories about magic. This is the very hypocrisy Jesus condemns. I suspect that in the Corinthian church there may have been religious leaders who inflamed the meat-eating issue in order to gain power and social standing.

Again, it is important to keep in mind that eating together was not simply about consuming food or the nature of food consumed. Sharing a meal meant eating off of the same plate, literally breaking a loaf of bread and handing part of it to someone else. Eating together was a sign of peace. Excluding someone from the table was a way to enforce social barriers.

This is exactly what Paul accuses Peter of doing in his letter to the Galatians. He relates an incident that's exactly the opposite of what happens between Peter and Cornelius:

> But when Cephas [Peter] came to Antioch, I opposed him to his face, because he stood self-condemned; for until certain people came from James, he used to eat with the Gentiles. But after they came, he drew back and kept himself separate for fear of the circumcision faction. And the other Jews joined him in this hypocrisy, so that

even Barnabas was led astray by their hypocrisy. But when I saw that they were not acting consistently with the truth of the gospel, I said to Cephas before them all, "If you, though a Jew, live like a Gentile and not like a Jew, how can you compel the Gentiles to live like Jews?" (Gal. 2:11–14)

Paul is incensed at Peter's hypocrisy. This is a clear example of partiality, of wearing a mask and play-acting. Paul accuses Peter of playing both sides, of kowtowing to the faction of Christians who insist on the enforcement of food regulations at common meals.

Which, by the way, is also exactly what Paul is proud of doing! Remember what he said in his letter to the Corinthians? "Give no offense to Jews or to Greeks or to the church of God, just as I try to please everyone in everything I do, not seeking my own advantage, but that of many, so that they may be saved." Both Peter and Paul have to navigate a delicate diplomatic issue in these new Christian communities.

I sympathize with them both. In my ministry, I've had to mediate between all kinds of disagreeing groups who were ready to come to blows over these things: a painting of Jesus hung in the sanctuary, the presence of projector screens in worship, the use of electric guitars, how to treat members who have committed crimes, how to treat families of victims, how to extend welcome to people of other races and sexual orientations or sexual identities, whether to use ancient language in creeds, the church's official stand on war, health care, local tax policy, and the Alabama Constitution. I believe there are right answers to some of these questions and nuanced answers to others, but I believe Paul is correct to point out that our positions on these things can also function as masks. Having the "right answer" puts us in an elite and exclusive social group. How do we respond in love while remaining firmly committed to our principles? The Christians who were committed to food regulations in the early church had a depth of history and firm belief in the rightness of those laws. How could Paul create a situation that encouraged them to stretch their minds? What theological principle would override their fear of eating next to a bacon-eating Gentile? The church had an answer: "God shows no partiality."

We know what finally happened. Decades after the controversy in Corinth, Mark would tell the story of Jesus saying that all the food that goes through us, clean or not, becomes excrement and goes into the sewer. Luke would tell the story of Peter visiting Cornelius and declaring that "God shows no partiality." We can see in Paul's writing the origins of the conflicts that would give this slogan momentum. Soon, every Christian would know it by heart.

CHAPTER 3:

FAITH AND FORESKINS

Listen! I, Paul, am telling you that if you let yourselves
be circumcised, Christ will be of no benefit to you!
...I wish those who unsettle you would castrate themselves!
Gal. 5:2, 12

Joining the Church

Imagine that you are a young man living in first-century Asia Minor. You
work as a clerk in your family's cloth business. You spend your free time
at the theater or watching sporting events at the arena. On holidays, your
family sacrifices an animal at one of the local temples, and you savor the
smell of roast meat as you and your male friends recline around the table
for dinner. You've been raised as a good citizen of the empire, so sometimes
you burn incense to Caesar as a sign of your patriotism.

But then you fall in with a group of people who worship a Jewish
prophet named Jesus. They tell the story of this itinerant rabbi who became
a thorn in the side of both the religious leaders and the government, of
his words which were both scandalous and true, and of the miracles he
performed. They tell the story of his crucifixion and resurrection, and they
believe that he has inaugurated a new era. One day, they say, he will return
to establish his new kingdom. They use the same words that you have heard
describe the emperor—Savior of the World, Son of God, born of a virgin—
but in their creeds it has a different meaning.

One of the most remarkable things about them is their community,
which is like none you've ever experienced. When they gather to worship
at someone's house, the world turns upside-down and inside-out. Slaves

and free people call each other "brother" and "sister." Poor people recline at the table while rich people serve the food and wash their feet. Not only are women allowed at the table, but they speak in public as freely as men. When someone has a crisis, the members of the community pool their resources, sell their property, and pitch in to help. This community, they say, is a preview of the kingdom of God, the way God intended the world to be from the beginning. They call themselves an *ekklesia*, an assembly of those God has "called out" to be an example of this kingdom. People genuinely love each other and they say that this crucified and resurrected Jesus is alive in them and among them.

After sharing their meals and taking part in this community, one day you decide you want to be one of them. You sit down with some of the leaders of this *ekklesia* and say that you've never felt so alive as when you are with them worshiping God, that it has changed your life, that you are ready to become a follower of Jesus and you are ready to be baptized.

They all smile and congratulate you. One by one they embrace you and kiss both cheeks. Then one of the leaders approaches you. You see the blade of a three-inch knife glinting in the lamp light. He smiles at you and says, "Well, let's go ahead and get you circumcised."

"What?" you ask.

"Circumcised," he answers. "It's when we cut off the foreskin of your penis."

You look into the faces of the men around you. They look at you expectantly. You stammer, "But what does my foreskin have to do with becoming a disciple of Jesus?"

"Jesus followed the Law of Moses," one patiently answers, "which very clearly requires circumcision. If you want to follow Jesus, you have to follow Moses first."

Seeing your reluctance, another tries to explain. "Look," he says, "Jesus suffered and died on a cross. He underwent terrible suffering. This is just a quick snip, a brief period of unimaginable agony for about a day, and then you'll heal up in a week or so. What does that compare with the suffering of martyrdom? You've heard the stories of Stephen, how he was stoned to death in Jerusalem. Circumcision is nothing compared to that. Think of this as your cross to bear. Don't you love Jesus enough to cut off this little piece of yourself?"

The Circumcision Crisis and the Jerusalem Council

This, in a nutshell, was the crisis the early church faced about circumcision. The issue crops up in Acts, Romans, Corinthians, and Galatians. A group of Christians was advocating that to be true followers of Jesus, male members should alter their male members.

Now, as you can imagine, this was a deal-breaker for a lot of would-be Christians. It seemed unfair to the Gentiles for a couple of reasons. First, only half the population—the male half—had to follow this law. Female converts only had to be baptized. Second, most Jewish Christians (like the first disciples) had been circumcised as infants. It had been decided for them when they were born. New adult converts who were Gentiles, though, were able to experience the full effect of terror and pain as they faced first-century surgery.

Like clean and unclean foods, this particular problem shows up so often in the New Testament that it is astonishing that modern Christians know almost nothing about it. In the story of Peter and Cornelius from Acts 10, the text highlights one of the big differences between the Jewish Christians and the new Gentile converts: "The *circumcised* believers who had come with Peter were astounded that the gift of the Holy Spirit had been poured out even on the Gentiles" (Acts 10:45; italics added).

In the very next chapter, Acts 11, Peter faces the consequences for meeting with and baptizing Cornelius and his household. "When Peter went up to Jerusalem, the *circumcised* believers criticized him, saying, 'Why did you go to *uncircumcised* men and eat with them?'" (Acts 11:2–3; italics added). Again, the language of Acts points out that it is not only food, but also the fact that the Gentiles had foreskins that was particularly objectionable. The idea of sitting down next to a man who still had his foreskin and casually eating a meal was shocking. If this doesn't call to mind images of American racial segregation, it should!

According to Acts, as the early church grew, more and more Gentiles joined the movement. In Antioch, large numbers of Gentiles became

Jesus-followers and people began to call them "Christians" (Acts 11:26). The new Gentile converts caused a crisis in the church's identity. Would new members have to become Jewish converts and be circumcised before they could become Christians?

The crisis reaches a climax in chapter fifteen of Acts, when the church in Jerusalem holds a council to decide what must be done.

> Then certain individuals came down from Judea [to Antioch] and were teaching the brothers, "Unless you are circumcised according to the custom of Moses, you cannot be saved." And after Paul and Barnabas had no small dissension and debate with them, Paul and Barnabas and some of the others were appointed to go up to Jerusalem to discuss this question with the apostles and the elders. So they were sent on their way by the church, and as they passed through both Phoenicia and Samaria, they reported the conversion of the Gentiles, and brought great joy to all the believers. When they came to Jerusalem, they were welcomed by the church and the apostles and the elders, and they reported all that God had done with them. But some believers who belonged to the sect of the Pharisees stood up and said, "It is necessary for them to be circumcised and ordered to keep the law of Moses." (Acts 15:1–5)

There are a couple of important things to notice about this passage. First, people came from Judea (where the church started) to Antioch. The Judean party was likely comprised of old-school Christians, people who had grown up Jewish or near Jewish culture, who knew their Hebrew Bible backward and forward. They may have regarded these Antioch Christians as newcomers, and when they found out that they were worshiping Jesus without understanding Jesus's own native culture, they probably felt like the Antioch Christians were lightweights, with a watered-down gospel, who didn't fully understand all the nuances and power of Jesus's life, death, and resurrection. Without circumcision, how could they understand the covenant? How could they understand the call to a holy heart and life, with

God's law written on their hearts? Where was the sign of their commitment to the radical lifestyle the Christian movement demanded?

The second thing to notice is that there are *Pharisees* who are *Christians* (15:5). The gospels portray Pharisees as the bad guys, the ones Jesus debates over and over again. What this story may capture is the point at which Pharisees *became* the bad guys for the early church.

Jesus belonged to the same rabbinical tradition as the Pharisees and had probably studied with Pharisee scholars. His contemporaries may have even regarded him as a Pharisee.[24] The early Jesus movement shared a lot in common with the Pharisees, including a devotion to God that spilled over into every area of life, a passionate desire to live a life that was holy.

If this crisis in the early church was framed as a debate between the procircumcision faction and the anticircumcision faction, then it may have left lingering resentment toward the Christians who were Pharisees. Even if there were Christian Pharisees who were tolerant of uncircumcised believers, over time the two groups came to be associated with each other. Eventually "Pharisee" came to mean, by definition, one who was intolerant of uncircumcised Gentiles.

The stories in the gospels may have been shaped by memories of this argument, so that the Pharisees come off not as close cousins of Jesus, but as his enemies. This is why in Matthew's gospel, Jesus goes on a chapter-long rant in which he repeatedly calls scribes and Pharisees hypocrites and snakes, saying that they tie up heavy burdens for others without lifting a finger to help them, and that they travel the world to make converts and then make them children of hell, and that they lock people out of the kingdom of Heaven (Matthew 23:1–15). While it is possible that this is a verbatim transcript of a real Jesus rant, it seems unlikely that this would represent Jesus's usual interactions with the Pharisees—especially if he had Pharisee followers! More likely, this tirade reflects the arguments going on inside the church at a critical point in its growth.

---

24 See Hyam Maccoby, *Revolution in Judaea: Jesus and the Jewish Resistance* (New York: Taplinger, 1981). Also Hyam Maccoby, *Jesus the Pharisee* (London: SCM Press, 2000).

After Paul and Barnabas relate their experience among the Gentile converts, Peter and James and the other leaders of the Jerusalem church agree that circumcision will not be a requirement for membership in the new community. Peter stands up and makes his speech:

> "My brothers, you know that in the early days God made a choice among you, that I should be the one through whom the Gentiles would hear the message of the good news and become believers. And God, who knows the human heart, testified to them by giving them the Holy Spirit, just as he did to us; and in cleansing their hearts by faith he has made *no distinction* between them and us. Now therefore why are you putting God to the test by placing on the neck of the disciples a yoke that neither our ancestors nor we have been able to bear? On the contrary, we believe that we will be saved through the grace of the Lord Jesus, just as they will." (Acts 15:7–11; italics added)

Peter appeals to the idea that God shows no partiality, no distinction between Jews and Gentiles. God pours out the Holy Spirit on both groups without making any distinction about whether or not they have foreskins.

Peter also refers to a yoke that many were not able to bear as adult males: the cutting of their own foreskins. He emphasizes that if the church requires circumcision, they are asking Gentiles to suffer through something most adult Jewish men had not. Peter's words sound very similar to Jesus's own when he accuses the Pharisees of tying up heavy burdens and laying them on the shoulders of others, yet being unwilling to lift a finger to move them (Matt. 23:4). Circumcision was a burden laid on the shoulders of *others,* not carried by those who were most insistent about the practice.

The author of Acts goes on to say that the Jerusalem leaders next compose a letter to the church in Antioch which informs them of their ruling: it is okay to be a Christian and keep your foreskin. They have decided on the full inclusion of Gentiles in the life of the church.

A Brief History of the Foreskin

I opened this chapter with an absurd story about a terrified man who hears the words "it's when we cut off the foreskin of your penis." When I've told this story in church, people are uncomfortable with the fact that I use the word "penis." I use it for shock value because most modern Christians seem to be able to talk about circumcision without ever acknowledging that they are talking about penises. In church, we'll read excerpts from Paul's letter to the Colossians, where he speaks of "spiritual circumcision" (2:11). Because Christians are not aware of this history, nobody ever actually explores the analogy. Do our spirits need circumcision? Is there something painful about our conversion? Are we marked in our spirits in some way with the sign of God's covenant? Is there something about our spirits associated with pleasure, or with nakedness, or with embarrassment? As with food regulations, Christians simply don't think about it because it is not an integral part of our religion. The shape and appearance of the male genitals is not of concern to us.

But it was to people of Jesus's day. Those who were descended from ancient Israelites had over a thousand years of circumcision history. They knew the way a circumcised penis was supposed to look, yet they lived amid the uncircumcised phallic imagery of Greek and Roman culture. It was everywhere: in phallic jewelry, statuary, and mosaics that today sit in museums all over the world. Men would gather at Roman baths to conduct business, where it was very clear who was and who was not circumcised. The Greeks and Romans were very fond of the foreskin, and considered it part of the natural beauty of the male form. Some Jews apparently sought to fit in better by having some form of reverse-circumcision.[25] They would try to stretch the remnant of their foreskin with weights or minor surgery to cover the glans of the penis. Paul mentions this practice in his letter to the Corinthians. He wants to deflect attention away from the foreskin and toward the kingdom of God:

---

25 "So they built a gymnasium in Jerusalem, according to Gentile custom, and removed the marks of circumcision, and abandoned the holy covenant. They joined with the Gentiles and sold themselves to do evil." (1 Macc. 1:15)

> Was anyone at the time of his call already circumcised? Let him
> not seek to remove the marks of circumcision. Was anyone at the
> time of his call uncircumcised? Let him not seek circumcision.
> (1 Cor. 7:18)

As I mentioned in the last chapter, one of the martyr stories in Maccabees describes how two mothers who circumcised their infant sons were
marched naked through the streets to their deaths. People's ancestors
died for their circumcision and their refusal to abandon their culture or
their God. Circumcision, no less than food regulations, was part of Jewish
national identity.

How can we read these ancient texts as though penises do not exist?
How can we read the scriptures as though circumcision can exist as an
abstract concept, apart from male genitals? Certainly it would be a mistake
to focus exclusively on biology, as though there were not some kind of spiritual or cultural meaning as well, but modern people need to be reminded
when they read the Bible that it was written by a male-dominated culture
that was very concerned with penises, reproduction, and power.

Modern people have diverse views on the history of circumcision. Some
believe that it is a cruel and unnecessary practice imposed upon infants.
They read the whole history of circumcision in a negative light, arguing that it has its origin in negative attitudes toward sexuality, or that it
is symbolic of human sacrifice. Most scholars agree that its origins, like
most social practices, are ambiguous. It has been rigorously analyzed from
anthropological, psychological, and theological perspectives.[26] In some cultures it functions as a rite of passage and is performed on older boys. In Jewish culture, though, it functions as a marker that this male child belongs to
this particular group, Israel, which has a covenant with God.[27]

In Genesis 17, it is a reminder of God's covenant with Abraham. God
promises Abraham that his descendants will inherit the land of Canaan,

---

26   See John Goldingay, "The Significance of Circumcision," *Journal for the Study of the
Old Testament* 88 (2000).
27   Nicolas Wyatt, "Circumcision and Circumstance: Male Genital Mutilation in Ancient
Israel and Ugarit," *Journal for the Study of the Old Testament* 33, no. 4 (2009), 412.

and that circumcision will be the sign of this agreement. Circumcision as a reminder of this promise makes a certain kind of sense: the male reproductive organ is marked with a reminder of the promise that descendants come from God.

It may also have something to do with human sacrifice.[28] There is a strange story in Exodus about how God attacks Moses without warning (Exod. 4:24–26). His wife, Zipporah, circumcises their son, then touches the bloody stone knife to Moses's penis.[29] God relents and lets Moses go. Why does God attack Moses? Is it because Moses is uncircumcised? Because his son is uncircumcised?[30] Moses should have been circumcised in the courts of Egypt, since the Egyptians also performed circumcision; maybe Moses's circumcision was incomplete or improperly done.[31] The whole book of Exodus has overtones of child sacrifice, of killing the firstborn as an offering to God. Sacrificing the firstborn in some ancient cultures, including the culture of ancient Egypt, was a way to protect subsequent children. Similarly, circumcision could have been a way of protecting people against unpredictable divine wrath.

For ancient people, fertility, sexuality, and death were linked. They lived with the ever-present threat of famine and infant mortality. Their lives depended on the fertility of their crops, their livestock, and their households. This is why throughout the Hebrew Bible, the ancient Israelites always seem to dabble with the worship of gods and goddesses of fertility. According to the prophets, they make love under sacred trees and worship at giant phallic pillars, monuments to fertility on hills scattered around the land (Isa. 57:5, Jer. 3:6). This may also be why God chooses Abraham and Sarah, an elderly infertile couple, to be the ancestors of God's new nation. God demonstrates that God alone, YHWH, the God of Israel,

---

28   See Omri Boehm, "Child Sacrifice, Ethical Responsibility and the Existence of the People of Israel," *Vetus Testamentum* 54, no. 2 (2004).

29   The text actually says "feet," but most scholars believe this is a euphemism for his genitals. See also Ruth 3:7–8.

30   Goldingay, "The Significance of Circumcision," 11.

31   Egyptian circumcision involved slitting the foreskin, whereas later Jewish practice involved total removal. See Jack M. Sasson, "Circumcision in the Ancient near East," *Journal of Biblical Literature* 85, no. 4 (1966).

is the god of fertility—not Baal or Astarte or any of the other Canaanite deities. When God announces that they will have children, Sarah laughs, asking the provocative question, "After I have grown old, and my husband is old, shall I have pleasure?" (Gen. 18:12). It is hard to tell which sounds funnier to her: the idea of having a baby, or the idea of having sex with Abraham again. Surrounded by phallic pillars and symbols of fertility, circumcision may have been a reminder that descendants come from the God of Israel, and not any other gods. It was a connection between them and the promise God made their ancestors.[32]

Circumcision, just like food regulations, was a source of national pride and national prejudice. Hundreds of years after Abraham, when the squabbling tribes of Israel were uniting under King Saul and King David, they referred to their enemies the Philistines (among others) as simply "the uncircumcised" (1 Sam. 14:6). When David comes to fight Goliath, he asks, "Who is this uncircumcised Philistine that he should defy the armies of the living God?" (1 Sam. 17:26). Later on, Saul asks David for an unusual bride-price for his daughter's hand in marriage: a hundred foreskins of the Philistines.

This emphasis on the appearance and function of the genitals also makes sense of some of the regulations about who is and is not allowed into the temple. One whose penis has been cut off, or who has deformed genitals, or who has been castrated, is not allowed into the temple (Lev. 21:20, Deut. 23:1). Such a person has been literally "cut off" from having descendants. He cannot participate in the covenant of Abraham, because he cannot bear descendants who will inherit the land.

It may seem cruel that a person who was castrated, perhaps as a prisoner of war or as a government official, would be doubly penalized by being banned from participating in the worship of God in the temple. When

---

32   For this reason, Abraham and, later, his grandson Joseph both say to men who swear oaths to them, "Put your hand under my thigh" when they make their promises (Gen. 24:2–3, 47:29). Instead of laying their hand on a Bible, they ask them to put their hands on their genitals, effectively swearing by all their descendants that have yet to be born. It is important to think of circumcision in light of this cultural reverence for the male organ. See Teresa Hornsby, *Sex Texts from the Bible: Selections Annotated & Explained* (Woodstock, NY: SkyLight Paths, 2007), 6–7.

Babylon conquered Jerusalem in 587 BCE and carried off the people into exile, it is likely that some of their men (perhaps including Daniel) were castrated to serve as officials in the Babylonian empire. Perhaps Isaiah speaks to their grief and shame when he writes:

> Do not let the eunuch say, "I am just a dry tree." For thus says the Lord: To the eunuchs who keep my sabbaths, who choose the things that please me and hold fast my covenant, I will give, in my house and within my walls, a monument and a name better than sons or daughters; I will give them an everlasting name that shall not be cut off. (Isa. 56:4–5)[33]

Even those who are banned from the sanctuary have a place in the sanctuary. God's impartiality trumps even the holiness code. The fact that their testicles are cut off does not mean that their heritage will be cut off.

An Angry Letter
Second-Class Christians

The complicated religious history of circumcision meant trouble for the Christian movement, where Jewish identity and the future of the Christian church were at stake. Even after the Jerusalem Council handed down its decision that Gentiles would be welcomed into the fold, Paul continued to argue with procircumcision Christians. It seems that circumcision became a marker for going the extra mile, or going above and beyond the call to normal discipleship. People who were truly dedicated to Jesus, who were ready to take up their cross and suffer for the gospel, could be pressured to bleed the way Jesus bled, to reach spiritual clarity (and superiority) by suffering. Those who were really dedicated could even castrate themselves and live celibate lives.[34] It was apparently an ongoing issue that kept cropping

---

33 Some scholars speculate that "eunuch" in this case (the Hebrew can also mean "court official") may refer to homosexuals. There is a wealth of literature, too much to explore here, on eunuchs and their function as officials, and what the Hebrew, Aramaic, and Greek terms for them mean. Hornsby, *Sex Texts from the Bible*, 76–79.

34 Christian self-mutilation was apparently widespread enough that church leaders sought to outlaw its practice. J. David Hester, "Eunuchs and the Postgender Jesus:

up enough that Paul felt it necessary to address it in several of his letters. The angriest and most pointed of these is his letter to the Galatians.

We can reconstruct from Paul's argument that a procircumcision group has been at work among the Galatians. I don't think it's difficult to imagine the kinds of rhetoric the procircumcision group uses to gain a foothold in the early church. "It's great that you want to follow Jesus," they might say, "but if you are really dedicated, if you really want to understand the mysteries of the universe and the will of God, you need to be circumcised." These people are not being merely legalistic. Adding requirements or making distinctions among levels or ranks in a religious hierarchy still appeals to people today. Paul faces the same kind of issue among the Corinthians, some of whom feel that Christians who speak in tongues or have certain spiritual gifts are superior to neophytes. First-class believers are those who go the extra mile, who bear the extra burden, who demonstrate their faithfulness or devotion in some extraordinary way. It's easy to imagine that those who choose to be circumcised feel a certain sense of accomplishment. They have demonstrated to their brethren and themselves that they are willing to make hard decisions and face physical pain to show their devotion. They may even feel a smug superiority to "baby" believers who have not yet made the final cut.

Paul has harsh words for people who think this way. His letter begins not with the typical wishes of well-being, or thanksgiving for friendship, but with "I am astonished that you are so quickly deserting the one who called you in the grace of Christ and are turning to a different gospel" (Gal. 1:6). He immediately turns to condemnation for the procircumcision faction, and to make sure he's perfectly clear, he says it twice: "If anyone proclaims to you a gospel contrary to what you received, let that one be accursed!" (1:9).

By setting up circumcision or speaking in tongues as a badge of honor and a mark of distinction among first-class and second-class Jesus-followers, the Galatians and Corinthians are trying to import the human tendency to create hierarchies into God's kingdom. As N. T. Wright says, "To undergo

Matthew 19.12 and Transgressive Sexualities," *Journal for the Study of the New Testament* 28, no. 1 (2005).

circumcision is, in effect, to give in to the principalities and powers. It is to step back into a scheme of blood, soil, race, and tribe. It is like going back to the paganism renounced at conversion."[35] These Christians think they are going forward in the faith, when they are really going backward.

A Credibility Problem

The procircumcision faction has not only been promoting circumcision, but also talking about Paul behind his back. For the next several paragraphs, Paul is on the defensive. Again, we can only speculate what they may have been saying. "Sure, Paul didn't tell you the truth about circumcision," they may have said, "because he's not a real apostle. He didn't walk with Jesus, the way Peter and James and others of us did. He's a Johnny-come-lately to the Christian movement, and when he was here he gave you his version of Christianity Lite. But, you know, some Christians are like that—always compromising in order to make their gospel more appealing to the masses." Perhaps they accused people of turning to Paul because he was a teacher who "suited their own desires" (1 Tim. 4:3).

We get a snippet of this kind of rhetoric in Acts, when Paul visits the church in Jerusalem and meets with James and the elders. They tell Paul,

> You see, brother, how many thousands of believers there are among the Jews, and they are all zealous for the law. They have been told about you that you teach all the Jews living among the Gentiles to forsake Moses, and that you tell them not to circumcise their children or observe the customs. (Acts 21:20–21)

The accusations have grown. Now, they claim, Paul is not merely peddling a "gospel lite" to baby Christians, he is actively telling people *not* to observe the law. He is encouraging them to assimilate and turn away from their religious heritage.

This is a perpetual problem for anyone involved in ministry. Rumors begin and words get twisted as debaters create straw men and mischaracterize

---

35   N. T. Wright, *What Saint Paul Really Said* (Cincinnati: Eerdmans, 1997), 137.

the motivations of their opponents. For Christians who preach tolerance and nuanced interaction with their surrounding culture, this means being characterized as enemies of the gospel, of watering down their religion, or of abandoning the distinctive witness of Christianity. For Paul, telling Gentiles that they don't have to be circumcised in order to follow Jesus gets turned into a point of doctrine, and suddenly rumors begin to spread that he is an enemy of Jewish practice, someone who tells Jews not to circumcise their children.

So Paul responds:

If anyone proclaims to you a gospel contrary to what you received, let that one be accursed! Am I now seeking human approval, or God's approval? Or am I trying to please people?

...You have heard, no doubt, of my earlier life in Judaism. I was violently persecuting the church of God and was trying to destroy it. I advanced in Judaism beyond many among my people of the same age, for I was far more zealous for the traditions of my ancestors. But when God, who had set me apart before I was born and called me through his grace, was pleased to reveal his Son to me, so that I might proclaim him among the Gentiles, I did not confer with any human being, nor did I go up to Jerusalem to those who were already apostles before me, but I went away at once into Arabia, and afterwards I returned to Damascus. (Gal. 1:9–17)

Paul points out that his authority comes not from being commissioned by anyone from Jerusalem, but from God. He does not admit that Peter, James, or any other apostles are in positions of authority over him, or that he has somehow received his teaching from a corrupted or discredited source. He wants to show them that he does not say different things to different people and that he does not preach a "soft" gospel.

In the middle of his story, Paul drops a telling line. When he describes his relationship to Peter and James, he says, "from those who were supposed to be acknowledged leaders (what they actually were makes no difference to me; *God shows no partiality*)—those leaders contributed nothing to me" (1: 6; emphasis added). Paul believes that God does not care about human ideas of rank or hierarchy. Paul's authority does not come from Peter or James or anyone else but God. This notion, that God shows no partiality, lies behind not only his understanding of his own authority, but the whole argument of Galatians.

In order to prove how consistent he is, he goes on to relate the story of how he visited Jerusalem the first time after he had become a Christian. He says that at their conference there were "false believers secretly brought in, who slipped in to spy on the freedom we have in Christ Jesus, so that they might enslave us" (Gal. 2:4). Apparently some members of the procircumcision faction were playing politics at the council and trying to advance their agenda, or to demonstrate that Paul was a fake. But Paul says, "We did not submit to them, even for a moment." They put pressure on Titus, one of Paul's uncircumcised entourage, to be circumcised. Paul proudly states that "even Titus, who was with me, was not compelled to be circumcised, though he was a Greek" (2:3). Paul has established his credibility. He is not peddling a "gospel lite," but a robust theology of Christian freedom, which he preaches even under opposition from sneaky "false believers."

Paul neglects to mention another incident involving Timothy. In Acts 16:1–4, even after Gentile Christians have been given permission from the Jerusalem Council not to be circumcised, Paul *does* bow to political pressure from the circumcision faction. He has his secretary, Timothy, circumcised before they go to a region where people know Timothy's family. Timothy's mother is Jewish, but his father is a Greek. Timothy's identity as a Jewish or Gentile Christian is in doubt in the hometown. It's a practical and diplomatic decision: In order for them to be taken seriously by his own people, Timothy needs to be circumcised—in order for them to deliver the good news that it's okay not to be circumcised! They want to show that it's not because they are afraid of circumcision, or lack dedication, but because there is a bona fide theological reason not to impose circumcision on others. In this situation, Paul acquiesces so that he may have credibility among another group.

This reminds me of a 2005 documentary called *The Education of Shelby Knox*.[36] Shelby, a high school student in Lubbock, Texas, comes from a conservative Southern Baptist family. She has taken a vow of sexual abstinence until marriage. As a student leader, she joins the Lubbock Youth Commission, which begins to lobby the city for comprehensive sex education in schools. She faces all kinds of resistance from Christian abstinence-only proponents, but her strong moral background, her deep religious convictions, and the reluctant but loving support of her conservative parents convince her that comprehensive sex education is the best way to fight Lubbock's high teen pregnancy rate.

In one powerful scene, a church leader argues with her about her political activities. He implies that people who want to teach kids about safer sex are simply capitulating to the social pressure to have sex early. Knowing her conservative Christian background, he says, "I'm disappointed in you."

She fires back that the reason she is outspoken about comprehensive sex education is that she does have a religious family, that she has taken a vow of abstinence, but that other kids don't have those privileges. This is what gives her the moral authority to argue on behalf of her peers. The religious leader sits there in stunned silence.

Shelby argues not from a position of moral capitulation, but of personal integrity. She has gone the extra mile in order to earn credibility among conservative adults for the benefit of her peers. She lives out Paul's understanding of freedom. Though Paul believed he had a right to eat meat sacrificed to idols and live as a Gentile, he would continue to follow the Law of Moses so that he might have credibility among all groups. "Nevertheless, we have not made use of this right, but we endure anything rather than put an obstacle in the way of the gospel of Christ" (1 Cor. 9:12). She has limited her own freedom in order to grant freedom to others.

Timothy's choice to be circumcised as an adult is, I believe, a kind that most people are reluctant to make. He has chosen to do something in order to argue that it is *not* necessary. In order to buy credibility among religious peo-

---

36   Marion Lipschutz and Rose Rosenblatt, *The Education of Shelby Knox*, Incite Pictures, 2005.

ple, this is sometimes a necessary step. This is a controversial and potentially dangerous principle, but it may be one that many who argue for progressive religious values need to learn. In order to buy freedom for others, sometimes we have to sacrifice our own, in order to demonstrate that we do not have a personal stake in the argument. Some gay and lesbian clergy, for example, choose to remain celibate even while arguing for greater acceptance of gay and lesbian relationships. Rather than complicate their witnesses, they have chosen to sacrifice personal freedom to win freedom on behalf of others.

Works versus Grace

But Paul only has the harshest words for those who try to persuade others to be circumcised. "You who want to be justified from the law have cut yourselves off from Christ. You have fallen away from grace...." (Gal. 5:4) He even goes so far as to say, "I wish those who unsettle you would castrate themselves!" (5:12). These are some of the angriest words in the New Testament.

Paul also uses some of the most beautiful language in the New Testament to argue that it's all about grace, not about foreskins. "In Christ Jesus neither circumcision nor uncircumcision count for anything; the only thing that counts is faith working through love" (5:6). He says that in Christ, "there is no longer Jew or Greek, there is no longer slave nor free, there is no longer male nor female; for all of you are one in Christ Jesus. And if you belong to Christ, then you are Abraham's offspring, heirs according to the promise" (Gal. 3:28–29). Again, the principle that stands behind Paul's whole argument, behind his own authority and the inclusion of uncircumcised Gentiles in God's salvation, is that God shows no partiality.

Paul doesn't want to put a stumbling block before anyone who wants to follow Jesus. In Jesus Christ, all distinctions between people slip away. Whether you are in a position of power or subservience, whether you are circumcised or uncircumcised, or whether you have a penis at all is completely irrelevant. God shows no partiality.

We can imagine the response, though. "If men don't have to be circumcised," the procircumcision faction could argue, "then what else don't they have to do? This is a slippery slope: first we throw out circumcision, next we'll throw out all self-denial and sacrifice, marriage and gender identity, and wearing clothes!" Paul makes clear that he is not talking about an anything-goes lifestyle. He invokes the Shelby Knox principle: "You were called to freedom, brothers and sisters; only do not use your freedom as an opportunity for self-indulgence" (Gal. 5:13).

This is another perpetual problem for Christianity and for ministry. Christianity has always had to navigate between freedom and legalism, grace and law, faith and works. For some Christians, drinking alcohol is a sin. For others, it is a right. The antialcohol faction describes the proalcohol faction as libertines, and the proalcohol faction describes the antialcohol faction as prudes.

The fights and divisions themselves prove that people don't get it: "The works of the flesh are obvious: fornication, impurity, licentiousness, idolatry, sorcery, enmities, strife, jealousy, anger, quarrels, dissensions, factions, envy, drunkenness, carousing, and things like these" (Gal. 5:19–21). The list is so overwhelming, it's easy to miss that Paul is addressing the bigger picture, which is the fact that he even has to *write* such a letter: enmity, strife, jealousy, anger, quarreling, dissension, factions—all of which has been a result of *arguing about cutting the foreskin of the penis*. When Paul talks about "works of the flesh," he is not just talking about fleshly pleasures and easily recognized sins of a dissolute lifestyle: "cigarettes, whiskey, and wild, wild women."[37] He is also talking about religious attitudes that are overly concerned with things like foreskins and how to cut them off—these are *literally* works of the flesh. Both these religious attitudes and the libertine lifestyle they oppose are works of the flesh, and they result in strife and factions.

The Genitals of Gentiles

Isn't it amazing? Nearly two thousand years later we in the church are still arguing about genitals. Homosexuality, gender identity, gay marriage, and the ordination of homosexuals are all modern topics that cause enmity, strife, jealousy, anger, quarreling, dissension, and factions. Many Christians have tried to simply avoid talking about the issues involved, and others

---

37 Tim Spencer, "Cigareets, Whusky and Wild Women," BMI, 1946.

have picked up banners around which to rally. Yet it was a remarkably similar issue that defined the early church and caused its rapid growth.

Hear the similarity: The book of Leviticus says that it is an abomination for a man to lie with a man "as with a woman" (Lev. 18:22). Based on a narrow interpretation of this part of Law of Moses, members of various antihomosexuality groups assert that gay persons should not marry, should not be ordained, or should not be admitted to the fellowship of Christian churches. There are many, many more references in the Hebrew Bible to the importance of circumcision in separating God's chosen people from the abominable cultures of the pagans, yet Paul was able to reconcile the ancient Jewish covenant with what God was doing among Gentiles in his own day because he knew that "God shows no partiality."

Now, there are many nuanced positions and theological reasons people give for their opinions on doctrine and social policy regarding homosexuality. It is neither possible nor necessary to survey them all here. I only wish to draw a comparison between the circumcision crisis that faced the early church and the similar crisis of gender and sexuality that faces the church today.[38]

---

38 I am partial to Siker's take on the subject:

> Rather than making an analogy between homosexual persons and women and ethnic minorities, I believe a more appropriate constructive analogy, and certainly more appropriate than the alcoholism analogy, is to view homosexual Christians today in the same way the earliest (that is, Jewish) Christians approached the issue of including Gentile Christians within the community.
> ...While I understand the sense of moral revulsion that many heterosexual Christians today may have when they contemplate homosexual relationships, is it in essence much different from the moral revulsion that early Jewish Christians apparently felt when contemplating association with impure and unclean Gentile Christians? Was not their sense of betraying the longstanding and sacred truth of ritual purity in the face of Gentile inclusion similar to the sense of some heterosexual Christians today that to welcome gays and lesbians into the church along with their homosexuality is to betray God's revealed truth?

Jeffrey S. Siker, "How to Decide? Homosexual Christians, the Bible, and Gentile Inclusion as Model for Contemporary Debate over Gays and Lesbians," *Theology Today* 51, no. 2 (1994), 229–31.

Those who believe that homosexuality makes someone unclean, or that homosexuality is a sin, often assert that it is a behavior that can be changed or an orientation that can be reversed if someone has sufficient willpower. They make the same arguments as the procircumcision faction. "Look," they say, "just cut off this part of yourself, and then you will be acceptable to our community." Like the procircumcision faction, they argue that the frustration of celibacy is nothing compared to the suffering of Christ. Straight preachers who condemn homosexuality as sin are really telling gays and lesbians that denying their attraction to other people is just their cross to bear—even though heterosexuals don't have to bear this particular cross or lift a finger to help others with their burdens. For heterosexuals, as for Jesus's first followers, their sexual orientation and their circumcised status were decided for them before they were born.

Proponents of accepting homosexual ordination and marriage often focus on reinterpreting those scriptures used by opponents, namely the passages from Leviticus (18:22, 20:13) and from Romans (1:26–27). The verses from Leviticus, for example, are oddly specific about men taking the role of women; female homosexuality is not ruled out, nor are other kinds of male homosexual activity. For these reasons, it seems that the author is far more concerned with preserving the symbols of a man's social position than with what modern people think of as "sexuality," and the overriding concern is not forbidding certain sexual acts but preserving Israel as a community of justice that avoids idolatry and temple prostitution. The activity is described in English translations as an "abomination," which is a word which seems to indicate "something pagans do."[39] It is entirely reasonable to argue that these passages are concerned not with the morality of specific sex acts, but with the cultural identity of ancient Israelites. Israelites, who were concerned with making sure that everyone, rich and poor, had a day of rest, who constantly warned the rich not to exploit the poor, and who were suspicious of surrounding kingdoms and their petty tyrants, may have seen this law as a way to prohibit the sexual exploitation and shaming of other

---

39 Eating shrimp, too, is described as an abomination (Lev. 11:10), which puts us seafood lovers in the same boat as gay men.

men. Since they knew the pagan myths of the kingdoms around them, they wanted to contrast their God, YHWH, with the pagan gods who did commit bestiality, rape of males and females, and other crimes.[40]

Many Christians point to Romans 1:26-27, where Paul says that people in Gentile nations, who did not have the Law of Moses and who chose not to seek out the truth about God, gave themselves over to various kinds of "unnatural" sexual pleasures, men with men and women with women. Paul's rhetoric, as Leviticus does, focuses on the idolatrous activities of pagan nations. It is worth noting what was going on in Paul's world at the time. The emperors Tiberius, Caligula, and Nero had shocked their citizens with their outlandish and degrading sexual treatment of their subjects. They were famous for raping men and women and participating in "unnatural" sexual acts involving juveniles or multiple partners. One of Caligula's victims became his assassin, and he took the opportunity to mutilate his genitals. This may be what Paul has in mind to when he refers to "men imposing shame on men and receiving in their own bodies the penalty for such deviance" (Rom. 1:27).[41]

But the whole point of Paul's tirade is what comes next. He goes on to say that it is not the ignorant people of Gentile nations, but "you who pass judgment on others" who "have no excuse" (2:1). Ultimately, Paul says, it is not being Gentile or Jew that saves us from God's anger, but God's own grace. Why?

"Because God shows no partiality" (Rom. 2:11).

The very passage from Romans that modern Christians use to condemn homosexuality as sin is the one that summarizes Paul's lifetime of mission and ministry, doing his best to reconcile Jews and Gentiles in the early

---

40 "The text does not refer to the immorality, sexual misdemeanors, or other bad behavior of the foreigners, but to the evil statutes of their gods, which are to be contrasted with the good statutes of the God of Israel." Mary Douglas, "Justice as the Cornerstone: An Interpretation of Leviticus 18–20," *Interpretation* 53, no. 4 (1999), 343.

41 "As a description of the horrors of the imperial house...Paul's words actually seem restrained." Neil Elliott, Liberating Paul: *The Justice of God & the Politics of the Apostle* (Minneapolis, MN: Fortress, 1994), 194-95. Elliott's argument is substantially different from the one I'm making here. He points out that this was part of a larger argument by Paul against the "justice" of the Roman Empire. The translation is Elliott's own.

church. People who adhere to his condemnation of homosexuality without understanding the rhetoric of his argument fail to see the forest for the fore-skins. It isn't homosexuality that concerns Paul, but the cultural prejudice that one group has for the other. We always assume that it is those other people who are "full of envy, murder, strife...and gossip" (Rom. 1:20). The point he is making is that there is no "us" and "them." As bad as we believe the other to be, it is we who are without excuse when we pass judgment on them. Matthew's Jesus makes a similar point: do not judge others, for you will be judged by the same measuring stick (Matt. 7:1).

I believe that in the Romans passage, Paul simply uses a bad example to make his point.[42] This isn't the first time he has done so. For example, he tells slaves not to be concerned to seek their freedom (1 Cor. 7:21), and to be obedient to their masters (Eph. 6:5)[43] not because slavery is acceptable and just in God's sight, but because he didn't want to give anyone an excuse to blame the new Christian movement for upsetting the social order. He tells women that they should keep their heads covered[44] when they proph-ecy for similar reasons (1 Cor. 11:3–16), although three chapters later he (or

---

42   Douglas Campbell advances the theory that Romans 1:18–32 is actually a sarcastic parody of the teaching of a procircumcision faction in Rome. The rhetoric is so negative toward Gentiles that it seems unlikely Paul meant it to be taken at face value unless it is intended as hyperbole. Campbell asserts that this is the straw man that Paul wants to knock down—which would, I suppose, include the homophobic comments in 1:26–27. See Douglas Campbell, *The Deliverance of God: An Apocalyptic Rereading of Justification in Paul* (Grand Rapids, MI: Eerdmans, 2009).

43   The Pauline authorship of Ephesians is disputed.

44   Another possible interpretation is that rather than keep their heads covered, Paul means that their hair should be pinned up. Still another possible interpretation comes from Martin. His intriguing idea connects ancient medical theories to Paul's reasoning in this passage. Hair was thought to play a role in fertility, and a woman's long hair was thought to "draw up" semen into her body. As such, her hair functioned as an expression of her genitals, and so covering her hair in worship was a sign of modesty. Troy W. Martin, "Paul's Argument from Nature for the Veil in 1 Corinthians 11:13-15: A Testicle Instead of a Head Covering," *Journal of Biblical Literature* 123, no. 1 (2004). I wonder if discom-fort about homosexuality in churches is due to the same problem? Women's hair makes men think about sex, so they should keep it covered—isn't that the same kind of argu-ment some people make about homosexuality? That it should be "covered up" so that we don't think about sex?

a later editor) says that they should be completely silent (1 Cor. 14:33–35). While many people who claim to read the Bible literally do claim that women should submit to male authority in church and not teach or speak, I don't know many literalist Christians who say that slaves should stay slaves, or who insist that women should wear hats in church. Modern Christianity's interpretation of what Paul considers sin and not sin, appropriate and inappropriate is wildly inconsistent.

I think the questions for Christians who read Galatians today are: How are we different from those early Christians who professed to love and follow Jesus Christ, but couldn't bear the thought of breaking bread with someone who had a foreskin covering his penis? Do we really believe that God's grace is sufficient for salvation, or do we believe that being heterosexual makes a person more acceptable to God than anyone else? Isn't requiring someone to act as a heterosexual or remain celibate a "work of the flesh"? Is it not grossly unfair to require that someone else bear a burden like celibacy that I am unwilling to bear also? What would Paul say to our churches today about our treatment of homosexuals?

While homosexuals have gained some social acceptance in secular culture in America, transgender persons still face tremendous stigma. People who do not fit neatly into male or female categories cause the rest of us anxiety. Like lobsters, lepers, and eunuchs of the first century, they are "unclean," creatures who do not fit neatly into our filing system.

But just like Isaiah, Jesus affirms their place in God's kingdom:

There are eunuchs who have been so from birth, and there are eunuchs who have been made eunuchs by others, and there are eunuchs who have made themselves eunuchs for the kingdom of heaven. Let anyone accept this who can. (Matt. 19:12)

It is difficult to know exactly what Matthew's Jesus means here. The first statement sounds as though Jesus is acknowledging something many modern people have begun to realize: that people's gender identity may not match their biology. There are many reasons this may be so: people are sometimes born with ambiguous genitals, or without the equipment needed to reproduce; they may have male chromosomes or genitals, but they are able to pass as female, or vice versa; there may be a developmental problem with their primary sex characteristics (genitalia) or secondary sex characteristics (hair, voice, and body shape); their brain chemistry or gender identity may simply be substantially different from others of their assigned gender; or they simply may not be capable of or interested in producing offspring. Whatever the case, they do not fit into neat categories of *dimorphic* sexuality—our understanding that there are two genders and two appropriate sexual orientations.

Regarding his last category, those who have made themselves "eunuchs for the kingdom of God," the conventional interpretation of this sentence is that people who choose not to marry, settle down, and have families, but who dedicate themselves to mission and ministry, are like the eunuchs of the ancient world.[45] It may be simply that they are people who have chosen not to have children. Whatever the case, they are respected court officials in the kingdom of God. Rather than being shunned or condemned, rather than being considered "dry trees" who are cut off from the covenant, they have a gift. People who choose to adopt the family of humanity rather than bearing children of their own still have an eternal monument in the kingdom of God.

Eunuchs also may have found a special home in the new Christian movement. Acts 8:26–40 tells the story of the apostle Philip meeting and sharing the gospel with an Ethiopian eunuch. The Ethiopian asks to be baptized immediately, so Philip baptizes him in a ditch on the side of the road. If having appropriately-shaped genitals or fitting neatly into gender categories is no longer a criteria for being included in God's salvation, then a castrated foreigner baptized in a pond by the side of the road is as much a Christian as anyone else. The scandal of God's impartiality means that even someone considered unclean for reasons of sexuality or gender, someone who can't be permitted all the way into the temple in Jerusalem, still has

---

45   This is the most popular Christian interpretation of this passage, but there are other ways to read it. "Eunuch" did not necessarily mean chaste. Hester makes a strong case that in antiquity "eunuch" could denote any number of ambiguous genders or sexual orientations. See Hester, "Eunuchs and the Postgender Jesus."

a place at the table where Christians share the Lord's Supper. The last are first, and the first are last.

Why do the scriptures I've shared in this chapter not get preached? Why do most Christians read the entire New Testament without recognizing that there is a major shift happening within its pages in the way people think about circumcision, sexuality, and procreation? I believe one of the reasons Christian churches have maintained bias against homosexuals and transgender persons is that Christians have forgotten the importance of the idea that God shows no partiality. It is this slogan that allowed Christians with foreskins to share communion with circumcised Christians and that welcomed eunuchs into the worshiping community. Without this slogan, the Christian church might not exist at all. The radical impartiality of God opened the new Christian community to all sorts of people who never imagined they would have a place among "the chosen."

I suspect Paul, if he had grown up in the twentieth century instead of the first and were writing to our churches, would probably use similar language to the rhetoric in Galatians. He might have harsh words for leaders who put obstacles in front of gays and lesbians. Perhaps he would tell them to go castrate themselves, as he does in Galatians, or remain celibate themselves if they will not allow gays to marry. Or he might simply use the words of Jesus. He might say of those religious leaders, "They tie up heavy burdens, hard to bear, and lay them on the shoulders of others; but they themselves are unwilling to lift a finger to move them." Or, "Woe to you, hypocrites! For you lock people out of the kingdom of heaven. For you do not go in yourselves, and when others are going in, you stop them."

I will confess that I managed to get through a fairly liberal seminary and graduate school and retain most of my prejudices about homosexuals. It was the practice of ministry that changed my mind about the subject. So I have sympathy for religious leaders who are reluctant to accept homosexuals as fellow clergy, or to perform gay weddings, in the same way that I sympathize with the early Jewish Christians who were reluctant to admit uncircumcised Gentiles into their community. I do not use the word "hypocrite" lightly, because I still feel the sting of those words when I realize Jesus is addressing them to me as a religious leader.

We walk the same path Paul walked in negotiating how we will live as a community, but we have been trying to do it without remembering that "God shows no partiality." Perhaps we can also find inspiration in the beautiful language Paul uses to describe to us a vision of the way the church could be: "There is no longer Jew or Greek, there is no longer slave nor free, there is no longer male nor female; there is no longer gay or straight, for all of you are one in Christ Jesus."

CHAPTER 4:

FAITH AND WORKS

You do well if you really fulfill the royal law according to the scripture,
"You shall love your neighbor as yourself." But if you show partiality, you
commit sin and are convicted by the law as transgressors.
James 2:8–9

An Old Debate

Once again, I found myself in a conversation about social justice with an evangelical Christian who disagreed with me. The words were so familiar I could practically lip-sync to them. "Sure," she was saying, "I know that it's important that we do good works, feed the hungry, house the homeless, and so on, but the main job of the church is to spread the gospel of Jesus Christ, not to be a social service charity."

"What is the gospel, then?" I countered. "Jesus himself said that he had come to bring good news to the poor and to set free the oppressed."

"The good news," she said, "is that Jesus Christ was the ultimate sacrifice for our sins, and now we can have forgiveness for our sins if we believe with our hearts and confess him with our mouths as savior and Lord."

"And where do you hear Jesus say that?" I asked.

"Jesus says, 'I am the way, the truth, and the life, and no one comes to the father except through me,'" she replied.

"No, I mean where does Jesus say that the whole point of his ministry is to die for our sin so that we can believe in him and God can forgive us?"

"Paul says it," she said. "In Romans."

Ah, Paul, I thought. If only you could have peered down the centuries and see how your letters would have been used, perhaps you would have picked your words more carefully. After a lifetime of writing letters to churches in conflict, you knew how people behave. The "spiritual" look down on those who are not. The circumcised look down on those who are not. Those who eat clean food look down on those who do not. The rich look down on those who are not. We bring all the baggage of the secular world into the church: endless wars, ethnic hatred, class privilege, and religious exclusivity. You tried so hard to get people to see a different kind of kingdom. You spent a lifetime of mission and ministry playing diplomat to factions of fighting Christians. You knew that if we really believed in Jesus Christ and loved God with our whole heart and our neighbors (and enemies) as ourselves, we would be one with each other and one with him.

At this point, I knew the conversation was stuck. This debate is as old as the church itself: Evangelism or missions? Social justice or personal piety? Works-righteousness or cheap grace? Many thoughtful Christians shrug and avoid the tension by saying, "Both." But answering this way allows us to avoid dealing with the reason for the tension itself: the church has forgotten the principle of God's impartiality.

Paul's Purpose

As we have seen in the last two chapters, the early church operated on the principle that God shows no partiality. The first disciples, the Jewish followers of Jesus, experienced his resurrection and his ongoing presence among them. They believed that God had initiated a new age on earth and that God's kingdom would become a reality. The inclusion of Gentiles as baptized members of the community was simply an extension of Jesus's life, ministry, death, and resurrection. They saw in Jesus the image of the God who shows no partiality, whose purpose all along was to bring the God of Israel into relationship with every human being on the planet, both Jew and Gentile. Even though Isaiah had predicted Israel would become a light to the nations (Isa. 49:6), it would be the followers of Jesus, both Jew and Gentile, who would be "the light of the world" (Matt. 5:15). God had broken the kingdom open wide and invited everyone to the banquet, even the outcasts (Matt. 22:9–10).

The wideness of God's mercy created its own problems: Who was chosen and who was unchosen? What about the promises made to Israel? If anyone can have salvation through Christ, and if nobody has to follow the Law of Moses, what's the point of the law? You can hear the same consternation in modern debates about homosexuality or any other issue that divides the church. Where are the boundaries? If these people can get in, who can't? Why even bother with the Bible (or the Law) if we're going to interpret it so loosely?

Romans is Paul's attempt to answer these questions.[46] He had been working to reconcile these tensions for years. His whole lifetime of ministry was spent connecting the new Jesus movement that God was opening to *unchosen* Gentiles with the history of God's *chosen* people, the Israelites. In Romans, he attempts to move beyond the endless debates about circumcision, food, hair coverings, speaking in tongues, slave-master relations, marriage, and celibacy. He focuses on the one thing that binds Christians together no matter what opinions they hold on these hot-button issues: salvation in Jesus Christ, which God bestows not because we are circumcised or refuse to eat certain foods, but because of God's own grace poured out—impartially—on God's world:

> For we hold that a person is justified by faith apart from works prescribed by the law. Or is God the God of Jews only? Is he not the God of Gentiles also? (Rom. 3:28–29).

Part of the problem is that Christians often treat the Bible (and Paul's letter to the Romans) as a philosophical treatise.[47] We read the Bible and

---

46   And, perhaps, to inoculate the Roman church against the activity of "countermissionary" teachers who opposed Paul. See Campbell, *The Deliverance of God*, 506. It is more difficult to detect a specific party of anti-Pauline missionaries in Romans than in some of his other writings, but I suspect Paul knew from experience what kind of opposition he could expect.

47   Brian McLaren does an excellent job teasing out some of the problems with the history of our interpretation of Romans in dialogues between characters in his book *The Last Word and the Word After That*, which is about hell and its place in Christian doctrine. One character laments that Protestant Christians have viewed the whole Bible through the lens of Romans, rather than viewing Romans through the lens of the gospels. Romans has been interpreted by modern Christians to mean that faith—where faith means belief in certain doctrines about Jesus or accepting him as one's personal Lord and savior—is the central message of the Gospel, and that doing good deeds is secondary

abstract certain principles from it without thinking about how they functioned rhetorically among the people to whom they were addressed. In other words, we are more concerned with the abstract meaning than with the actual argument. Paul is writing a letter to particular people with particular concerns. He is not composing a multivolume work on systematic theology. When we forget to treat his letter as a letter, "faith" and "works" become abstract ideas that we talk about functioning in such-and-such a way. "Salvation" likewise becomes an abstract concept that we talk about as if it is a *thing* that we can *have*. When we remember that "salve" means healing, and connect it to the history of Israel and what "healing" meant to a population of people who saw their city destroyed and who faced persecution, assimilation, and annihilation for generations, then we can understand that "salvation" in a different way.

Once abstracted from their context, words like "faith" and "works" can be used in ways that other scriptures flatly contradict. I have even heard preachers assert that the good deeds done by those who are not in a relationship with Jesus are worthless to God, because we can never earn God's love, and compared with God's holiness "our righteous deeds are like a filthy cloth" (Isa. 64:6).[48] They interpret "works" to mean doing good deeds, performing right actions like feeding the hungry and housing the homeless. These deeds only have value, they argue, for one whose heart is already right with God through faith in Jesus Christ.

They are mistaken. When Paul uses the word "works," he has foremost in mind things like circumcision and food regulations, not good deeds done for the poor. Paul does not mean "good deeds," since, as he argues earlier, God will "repay according to each one's deeds" (2:6). Good deeds are evidence of God's law written on the hearts of human beings, regardless of whether they are Jew or Gentile:

---

or even irrelevant. See Brian McLaren, *The Last Word and the Word after That: A Tale of Faith, Doubt, and a New Kind of Christianity* (San Francisco: Jossey-Bass, 2005), 209.

48   It was only a few decades ago that Bailey Smith asserted that "God does not hear the prayer of a Jew." Kaylor, "Anniversary of Bailey Smith's Harmful Moment in Baptist-Jewish Relations."

When Gentiles, who do not possess the law, do instinctively what the law requires, these, though not having the law, are a law to themselves. They show that what the law requires is written on their hearts, to which their own conscience also bears witness; and their conflicting thoughts will accuse or perhaps excuse them on the day when, according to my gospel, God, through Jesus Christ, will judge the secret thoughts of all. (Rom. 2:14–16)

Paul anticipates a great unmasking, when God will judge the world. Whatever their status regarding belief in correct doctrines of God, regardless of their conflicting motivations for doing good, God will repay all according to their deeds. "What the law requires" is written on their hearts. If there is some question about their motivation or their "secret thoughts," God will sort it out in the end.

For Christians who believe salvation can only come through conscious acceptance of a formal doctrine about Jesus Christ, this passage is a real problem. The Gentiles Paul describes in his illustration do not only lack the law. They lack the gospel. There have always been "righteous Gentiles," according to Judaism, who fear God and do what is right.[49] These Gentiles are neither Jews nor Christians, yet Paul has just said that the law is written on their hearts, through their consciences, and that on the day of judgment their conflicting thoughts will "accuse or perhaps excuse them." Paul is talking about salvation in a way that would make many modern evangelicals condemn him for heresy. The impartiality of God means that God relates to human beings not on the basis of whether they know the law intellectually (or, I would argue, the correct doctrine about Jesus), but on the basis of the law in their hearts (their "secret thoughts") and their deeds.

Yet the Romans explanation of salvation by faith in Jesus Christ has become a standard way of explaining what Christianity is all about. Christians eager to convert others to Christianity pass out tracts that summarize "the Romans Road" to salvation. The word "evangelism" has become almost synonymous with getting people to accept this particular picture of salvation.

---

49   People like Ruth and Naaman (2 Kings 5) are examples of such people.

According to this theology, those who reject this understanding of salvation reject Christ, and those who reject Christ are destined for hell. For believers it is a powerful argument: Why would anyone reject the idea, if rejecting the idea meant that you would go to hell? It is a self-reinforcing and exclusive belief system. Those who believe this way are saved, and those who do not are damned. Because they have this narrow understanding of salvation, Christian exclusivists fear that anyone who diverts attention away from the primary mission of the church (which is getting other people to believe Christianity) is dangerous. Anyone who preaches social justice—or any Christian ethics that goes beyond individual salvation—is working for the devil.

Christians who critique exclusivism often use James as their go-to scripture. "Faith without works is dead" (James 2:17), they say, quoting scripture to argue scripture. They argue that following Jesus means "doing good works" so that others may "see and give glory to your Father in heaven" (Matt. 5:16).

The problem is that James and Paul aren't really disagreeing with each other. Paul did not write his letter to the Romans as an essay on how to get to heaven or as an abstract treatise on faith, works, and their relationship to salvation. He wrote it to explain the impartiality of God, how God was working to save the world, and how Jewish Christians and Gentile Christians could live together in the same community and interpret their history with reference to Jesus Christ. Everyone, Paul argued, Jew and Gentile alike, is saved by God's action in Jesus Christ. He was less interested in getting people to believe correct doctrine and more interested in getting diverse groups of people to get along and live together without disrespecting each other's faith backgrounds. So how did we get from Paul's letter to its modern interpretation?

The Letter to the Romans

Romans is probably one of the most thoroughly studied books of the Bible, and entire libraries of books are dedicated to its analysis. I do not intend to give a complete picture of what salvation means, but to show how the idea of God's impartiality works in it. A short sketch of the first few chapters is all we need to compare Paul's actual letter to the theology of Christian exclusivism.

I am a debtor both to Greeks and to barbarians, both to the wise and to the foolish—hence my eagerness to proclaim the gospel to you also who are in Rome. For I am not ashamed of the gospel; it is the power of God for salvation to everyone who has faith, to the Jew first and also to the Greek. For in it the righteousness of God is revealed through faith for faith; as it is written, "The one who is righteous will live by faith." (Rom. 1:14–17)

This is Paul's thesis. It is artfully composed. He refers to two elite groups, Jews and Greeks, some of whom suppose themselves culturally superior to the rest of the world. The Greeks had brought their enlightened culture and philosophy, their architecture and their mythology to the "barbarians" of other nations. There were two ways to do things: the Greek way and the barbarian way, civilized and uncivilized.

The Jewish culture likewise saw itself as different (and sometimes superior) to other nations. Paul, educated both in Greek philosophy and Jewish law, is a man of two elite worlds. Both traditions make judgments about the wisdom and folly of outsiders, but Paul has often found himself cast as a fool in both Greek and Jewish worlds because he preaches about the power of a crucified Jewish messiah: "For Jews demand signs and Greeks desire wisdom, but we proclaim Christ crucified, a stumbling-block to Jews and foolishness to Gentiles" (1 Cor. 1:22–23). Still, Paul says he is not ashamed of the gospel because "it is the power of God for salvation to everyone who has faith, to the Jew first and also to the Greek." You can hear in these verses the history of his mission and ministry, from his presence at the Jerusalem Council, where Gentiles were first admitted to the church without circumcision, to his debates with stoic and epicurean philosophers at Mars Hill in Athens (Acts 17:16–34). You can hear his conflict with the holier-than-thou faction of the Corinthians and the circumcising faction of the Galatians. In Romans, Paul is setting up another case for arguing God's impartiality.

For the wrath of God is revealed from heaven against all ungodliness and wickedness of those who by their wickedness suppress the truth. For what can be known about God is plain to them, because God has shown it to them. Ever since the creation of the world his eternal power and divine nature, invisible though they are, have been understood and seen through the things he has made.

So they are without excuse; for though they knew God, they did not honor him as God or give thanks to him, but they became futile in their thinking, and their senseless minds were darkened. Claiming to be wise, they became fools; and they exchanged the glory of the immortal God for images resembling a mortal human being or birds or four-footed animals or reptiles. (Rom. 1:18–23)

Paul begins by drawing a caricature of pagan religions. He could look around and see murals depicting Egyptian, Greek, Roman, or Phoenician gods and monsters from their mythologies, deities with bird-heads and lion heads, or who took the form of a bull or a swan to seduce young virgins.[50] In spite of their supposed wisdom, Paul argues, these pagans were foolish and perverse. Paul appeals to a feeling of cultural superiority, and pulls out all the stops in trying to create in his hearers a visceral reaction to "those people."

Roman Jews could understand the distinction their Bible made between Israel, which worshiped the unseen YWHW, and the antics of the pagan gods. Of course God would be angry at the nations! They had chosen to worship images of animals rather than the great I AM, and emulate the soap-opera antics of gods rather than the directives of the Creator. What Paul has done in this passage is to get his readers on board with his condemnation of pagan religion:

And since they did not see fit to acknowledge God, God gave them up to a debased mind and to things that should not be done. They were filled with every kind of wickedness, evil, covetousness, malice.

---

50   Zeus had a habit of seducing both women and men as animals: Leta he seduced as a swan, Europa he seduced as a bull, and Ganymede he seduced as an eagle. Things typically ended poorly for the mortals whom the gods loved.

Full of envy, murder, strife, deceit, craftiness, they are gossips, slanderers, God-haters, insolent, haughty, boastful, inventors of evil, rebellious towards parents, foolish, faithless, heartless, ruthless. They know God's decree, that those who practice such things deserve to die—yet they not only do them but even applaud others who practice them. (Rom. 1:28–33)

Now his hearers are cheering him on. "Yeah!" they say. "Those lousy pagans!" Which makes the next line all the more shocking.

Therefore *you have no excuse*, whoever you are, when you judge others; for in passing judgment on another you condemn yourself, because you, the judge, are doing the very same things. (Rom. 2:1; italics added)

Pow. Paul has pulled a deft rhetorical sleight-of-hand. He began by saying "They are without excuse," way up in 1:20. Now he has turned the tables and said, "You are without excuse" when you pass judgment on them. He has invoked the principle of God's impartiality, and it is a zinger.

You say, "We know that God's judgment on those who do such things is in accordance with truth." Do you imagine, whoever you are, that when you judge those who do such things and yet do them yourself, you will escape the judgment of God? Or do you despise the riches of his kindness and forbearance and patience? Do you not realize that God's kindness is meant to lead you to repentance? But by your hard and impenitent heart you are storing up wrath for yourself on the day of wrath, when God's righteous judgment will be revealed. For he will repay according to each one's deeds: to those who by patiently doing good seek for glory and honor and immortality, he will give eternal life; while for those who are self-seeking and who obey not the truth but wickedness, there will be wrath and fury. There will be anguish and distress for everyone who does evil, the Jew first and also the Greek, but glory and honor and peace for everyone who does good, the Jew first and also the Greek. For God shows no partiality. (Rom. 2:2–11)

For a letter that is supposedly about salvation by faith, this passage certainly emphasizes deeds. "He will repay according to each one's deeds," apparently regardless of whether one is Gentile or Jew. His vice list contains several minor infractions: "insolent, haughty, boastful," and so on, so that no one escapes.

All who have sinned apart from the law will also perish apart from the law, and all who have sinned under the law will be judged by the law. For it is not the hearers of the law who are righteous in God's sight, but the doers of the law who will be justified. (Rom. 2:12-13)

Paul establishes that both the "out-group" (Gentiles, or those who we consider wicked) and the "in-group" (the Jews, or, I would argue, us Christians) are held to the same standard. Of the out-group, he says, "they are without excuse" (1:20), because they had some inkling of God, though they did not have the written law. Of the in-group, he says "you have no excuse" (2:1), because we do the same thing. Toward the end of this argument, he states that "God shows no partiality," (2:11), and concludes, "When Gentiles, who do not possess the law, do instinctively what the law requires, these, though not having the law, are a law to themselves. They show that what the law requires is written on their hearts" (2:14–15).

Apparently, Paul argues, not all Gentiles of pagan nations are automatically rejected, nor are all Jews automatically accepted. Yet Christian exclusivists resist the same rhetoric applied to our own faith. There are atheists and people of other religions who act as though the law of God is written on their hearts, and there are Christians whose gossip, anger, judgment, and factionalism demonstrate that they have, at best, a flimsy grasp on "what the law requires."

According to Christian exclusivism, these observations are irrelevant, because all have fallen short of the glory of God and must have a relationship with Jesus Christ in order to have salvation. But if these observations are irrelevant, why does Paul make them? Why set up such a rhetorical trap in the first few pages of his letter?

He doesn't stop there:

> But if you call yourself a Jew and rely on the law and boast of your relation to God and know his will and determine what is best because you are instructed in the law, and if you are sure that you are a guide to the blind, a light to those who are in darkness, a corrector of the foolish, a teacher of children, having in the law the embodiment of knowledge and truth, you, then, that teach others, will you not teach yourself? While you preach against stealing, do you steal? You that forbid adultery, do you commit adultery? You that abhor idols, do you rob temples? You that boast in the law, do you dishonor God by breaking the law? For, as it is written, "The name of God is blasphemed among the Gentiles because of you." (Rom. 2:17–24)

In a stinging indictment, Paul says that, in contrast to the exemplary behavior of some Gentiles, the hypocrisy of the religious in-group dishonors the name of God: "The name of God is blasphemed among the Gentiles because of you."

I hear in this section the same sentiments expressed by non-Christians about their gripes with the church. Militant atheists gleefully point to Christian intolerance and hypocrisy as evidence that the very idea of God is toxic. George Barna's research found that the phrases most non-Christian young adults associate with the word "Christian" are "antigay," "judgmental," and "hypocritical."[51] While some of that perception is certainly due to negative stereotypes, it is still true that the biggest obstacle to spreading the Good News is Christians who are in love with bad news. People who know that God is love because God's law is written on their hearts recog-

---

51 David Kinnaman and Gabe Lyons, *UnChristian* (New York: Baker Books, 2007). Based on research from the Barna group.

nize that the version of Christianity they have heard goes against that law. Because God has given them a conscience, they reject an unconscionable God.

It's important to keep in mind that what Paul is doing here is rhetorical. He is arguing a point, trying to turn the tables on those who believe in their own religious, cultural, or moral superiority. This is why Paul goes on to specifically describe the circumcision issue, highlighting once again the tendency of religious people to obsess about symbolic expressions of piety:

> Circumcision indeed is of value if you obey the law; but if you break the law, your circumcision has become uncircumcision. So, if those who are uncircumcised keep the requirements of the law, will not their uncircumcision be regarded as circumcision? Then those who are physically uncircumcised but keep the law will condemn you that have the written code and circumcision but break the law. For a person is not a Jew who is one outwardly, nor is true circumcision something external and physical. Rather, a person is a Jew who is one inwardly, and real circumcision is a matter of the heart—it is spiritual and not literal. Such a person receives praise not from others but from God. (Rom. 2:25–29).

Again, Paul emphasizes God's impartiality, recognizing that God is less concerned with masks and appearances and more concerned with the heart. These uncircumcised Gentiles are "inward Jews"! Could Christians accept this same idea? That those who have rejected Christianity because they perceive it as antigay, judgmental, and hypocritical, may still be "inward Christians" because they love God with their whole heart and mind and love their neighbor as themselves? Could we, in a post-Christian culture, be surrounded by people who are inwardly Christian (and therefore also inwardly Jews)? Might it be that the church's proclamation of the gospel of Jesus has been so successful that many people who *really* understand Jesus have rejected the church in droves for its hypocrisy? Recognizing the consternation his approach may cause, Paul turns to some rhetorical questions to head off possible objections. Paul ponders the question, "What advantage has the Jew (3:1)?" "Are we any better off (3:9)?" We can hear the same objections and questions from Christians today. His answer can best be summed up as, "sort of." On the one hand, "the Jews were entrusted with the oracles of God" (3:2). There can hardly be an honor greater than this. On the other hand, "both Jews and Greeks are under the power of sin" (3:9). Paul reiterates that "there is no distinction [or partiality], since all have sinned and fallen short of the glory of God" (3:23) and rely on the grace of God for salvation.

Paul then turns from his rhetorical questions to the example of Abraham:

> What then are we to say was gained by Abraham, our ancestor according to the flesh? For if Abraham was justified by works, he has something to boast about, but not before God. For what does the scripture say? "Abraham believed God, and it was reckoned to him as righteousness." (4:1–3)

Abraham was not, technically speaking, Jewish. He lived hundreds of years before God delivered the law to Moses, yet God approached him and established a covenant for his descendants before he was ever circumcised. Paul proudly points to the passage in Genesis 15:6 that says, "Abraham believed God, and it was reckoned to him as righteousness" (4:3). Abraham gets credit for being righteous because he trusted God, Paul says. To make it clear that this pre-Jewish patriarch did not depend on his status as a Jew for his relationship with God, Paul asks, "How then was [righteousness] reckoned to him? Was it before or after he had been circumcised? It was not after, but before he was circumcised" (4:10)! In other words, Abraham had access to God's grace the same way that Gentiles all over the world now have access to it: through faith. The status of their foreskins (and their Jewishness) has no bearing on the issue.

In the rest of the letter Paul explores the implications of this new way of thinking about God. He wrestles with how to interpret the history of Israel and Jewish-Gentile relations in the church, he touches on predestination and free will, he laments the rejection of Jesus by religious leaders, and he expounds upon the ethical obligations of believers. While his heart breaks for Jews who have chosen not to follow Jesus, saying, "I could wish that I myself were accursed and cut off from Christ for the sake of my own people," (9:3), he believes that in the end, "all Israel will be saved" (11:26). Moreover, if God will save all of Paul's own people, God will likely save all the Gentiles, as well: "If [the Jews'] stumbling means riches for the world, and if their defeat means riches for Gentiles, then how much more will their full inclusion mean" (11:12)!

Throughout the letter, Paul highlights again and again the idea that God shows no partiality. "There is no distinction between Jew and Greek; the same Lord is Lord of all and is generous to all who call on him" (10:12). Different gifts and talents among believers do not mean that God makes distinctions, because "as in one body we have many members, and not all the members have the same function, so we, who are many, are one body in Christ" (12:5), a theme Paul has written on before (1 Cor. 12:12). The entire letter is a testament to the principal of God's impartiality that Paul has promoted his whole life.

The Romans Road

Paul's clear emphasis on God's impartiality in Romans is part of what makes Christian history so ironic. "Justification by faith, not by works" is an expression that, for most Protestant Christians, stands near the center of their belief in Jesus Christ. For the last several hundred years, theologians have regarded it as the indisputable product of a theological equation, just like $2 + 2 = 4$. The equation changes, though, if we understand that when Paul uses the word "works," he is thinking of something more like circumcision instead of something like immunizing children in developing world countries. Paul makes the case that Gentiles who do the latter have been motivated by a love for humanity that is close to God's own, and has shown that the law of God is written on their hearts. Gentile Christians who circumcise themselves, though, are motivated not by the law of God but by desire to be part of an in-group.

"Justification by faith" is such an important idea for modern Christians that to accuse someone of "works-righteousness" has the same weight as accusing them of heresy[52] or atheism. Unfortunately, it has also been used as a tool to resist change. Often when a renewal movement in the modern church begins to gather steam, when people have started living lives of radical discipleship, giving away their possessions, living in community, and preaching that Christians should live in a way that is significantly different from the surrounding culture, they face charges of promoting "works-righteousness." People who argue that Christians should feed the hungry, liberate the oppressed, and, in John Wesley's words, "do all the good they can by whatever means they can" will inevitably be accused of it. Opponents of change deploy this phrase any time they want to take the wind out of the sails Christian activists, as if heeding God's call to change the world were at odds with believing in God.

The faith equation has been reinforced by traditional Protestant interpretation of Romans. A good example of this interpretation is "the Romans Road," a series of scriptures pulled from Paul's letter to the Romans and used by evangelists to explain to prospective converts why they need Jesus. The Romans Road also demonstrates that how you slice a scripture, which passages you highlight and which words you emphasize, completely changes its meaning. It goes something like this:

1) We humans can never be holy enough for God. Nothing we can do will earn God's approval. "All have sinned and fallen short of the glory of God" (3:23).

2) Because of our sin we are destined for destruction. "For the wages of sin is death" (6:23).

3) But Jesus brings the gift of eternal life. "But the free gift of God is eternal life in Jesus Christ" (6:23).

---

52   The "Pelagian heresy" was named after Pelagius, a fifth-century monk who claimed, among other things, that there was no such thing as original sin, and that human effort could earn God's favor.

4) We have access to eternal life by believing the story of Jesus's death and resurrection. "If you confess with your lips that Jesus is Lord and believe in your heart that God raised him from the dead, you will be saved" (10:9).

I would never argue with the substance of these ideas. No one can earn God's approval, no matter how many elderly people they help across the street or how many poor children they immunize. We will work ourselves to death if we try to earn God's love, slaving away to our own guilt and psychological baggage. But this way of talking about salvation has more to do with the Protestant Reformation than with Paul or his concerns.

Martin Luther, who launched the Protestant Reformation, constantly beat himself up for never being worthy of God's love. One day he came to the realization that he didn't have to. When he read Paul's letter to the Romans, the idea that we are justified by faith, not by works, freed him from a lifetime of guilt and self-hatred.

He used this principle to fight against the corruption of the church in his day. Religious hucksters would promise people rewards in the afterlife for giving their money to the church. Martin fought against this corruption using scriptures from Romans, pointing out that salvation comes from God's grace through faith, not from donating money to the church or other "works of the flesh."

Martin's thinking has been an especially powerful theology among two groups of people. First, it has been a dominant theology for Christians who have felt terrified by the holiness of God, who carry around the weight of their guilt and an awareness of their own sinfulness. Hearing that we are justified by faith, not by works, brings people to the altar to lay hold of Jesus's love and God's amazing grace. Second, it has been a useful tool for Christian reformers who are suspicious of the hierarchy of the church. It gives them power to resist tyrannical church leaders. They relate to God with a personal faith, and not through a religious bureaucracy.

While those are laudable results of the doctrine, Paul had something very different in mind. When Paul wrote his letter to the Romans, he was doing so as a pastor who had spent a significant portion of his adult life settling disputes in Christian communities. As we have seen, the most contentious and pervasive disputes had to do with "how Jewish" the new Christian communities would be. Would they require people to avoid certain foods? Would they require new converts to observe Jewish holidays? Would new converts have to be circumcised?

These were not abstract theological questions, and they had nothing to do with what modern Christians tend to think of as "good works." Paul's letters addressed divisions in the community. If he did not speak up for them, those men who chose not to be circumcised would be second-class Jesus followers, and those who didn't abstain from unclean meat would be considered unclean human beings, unfit to be in the presence of superior Christians. Nearly every letter Paul wrote had some kind of church conflict behind it. There was always the threat that the church would split into those who followed the letter of the law and those who followed its spirit, between circumcised and uncircumcised, those who ate meat sacrificed to idols with their families on pagan holidays and those who remained steadfastly kosher, those who displayed more "spiritual" gifts like speaking in tongues and those who did not.

In these kinds of disputes about partiality, Paul came to rely on a simple theological premise: it's all about Jesus. It is God acting in Christ who saves us—not cutting the foreskin of one's penis, not eating kosher, not refraining from pagan meat, not keeping certain holidays. We might extend the concept: It is Christ who saves us—not being baptized a certain way, not refraining from alcoholic beverages, not saying "Merry Christmas" instead of "Happy Holidays," not being heterosexual. All of those things are "works," most of which are ways of claiming a certain identity within a social group.[53] Faith, on the other hand, has to do with our beliefs and actions that rest on our understanding of who God is and what God does. Christians have faith in Jesus because they see in him the shocking, amazing, powerful image of God. They see in a crucified messiah the love

---

53 "Paul has no thought in this passage of warding off a proto-Pelagianism, of which in any case his contemporaries were not guilty. He is here, as in Galatians and Philippians, declaring that there is no road into covenant membership on the grounds of Jewish racial privilege." Wright, *What Saint Paul Really Said*, 129.

of God for the very sinners who hammer nails through his body, and in a resurrected Christ the power of God that is stronger than death, religion, or empire. Confessing this Jesus as Lord means that we believe in a Lord who shows no partiality, who saves Gentiles as well as Jews, slaves as well as freemen, men as well as women. In fact, Paul holds out hope that God will save all of creation.

While Paul demolishes barriers between religions and cultures, and holds out the possibility of universal salvation, he doesn't believe that everyone is simply off the hook. This is usually the objection raised by people who feel threatened by the inclusive nature of the Good News: that if we allow people into the club who are not circumcised, or who eat meat sacrificed to idols, or who sleep with someone of the wrong gender, we are simply throwing out all standards of commitment, discipline, or morality. Paul repeatedly tries to head off such objections. "What then are we to say?" he asks. "Should we continue in sin in order that grace may abound? By no means! How can we who died to sin go on living in it" (6:1–2)?

Most direct is his prediction of judgment in the coming kingdom:

For he will repay according to each one's deeds: to those who by patiently doing good seek for glory and honor and immortality, he will give eternal life; while for those who are self-seeking and who obey not the truth but wickedness, there will be wrath and fury. There will be anguish and distress for everyone who does evil, the Jew first and also the Greek, but glory and honor and peace for everyone who does good, the Jew first and also the Greek. For God shows no partiality. (Romans 2:6–11)

In judgment, as in mercy, God shows no partiality. Just as people who act good demonstrate that the law of God is written on their hearts, regardless of their cultural or religious practice, people who do evil show themselves to be lawless, whether they live by the Law of Moses or not. God apparently judges both the good and the wicked impartially. The author of First Peter invokes the same idea: "If you invoke as Father the one who judges all people impartially according to their deeds, live in reverent fear during the time of your exile" (1 Pet. 1:17). Claiming Jesus as Lord and God as Father entails certain obligations on one's life. God has saved us from the power of sin and death; continuing to do evil would be like trying to breathe water after we had been rescued from drowning.

James's Letter

It did not take long for Paul's message to be distorted into a theology of cheap grace. Just a few years after he wrote Romans, Christians were latching on to key ideas about Jesus and declaring that these were the center of the Christian faith. James had to contend with the aftermath of Paul's revolutionary writing.

The central issue that seems to have prompted James's writing is class division. Perhaps there was an early version of the prosperity gospel circulating in these early churches. People may have been saying, like many modern popular preachers, that devotion to God would result in material blessings, that following Jesus would mean fat investment accounts and a life of ease. Or it may have simply been that some Christians felt that since the main thing was to get one's soul right with God that it was enough to preach to the poor that God would forgive their sins and give them a better life when they died. This tends to be the approach of some modern churches, which believe that social justice and working to empower poor people are at odds with "real" evangelism.

The first clue that James may have Romans in mind is in the introduction:

My brothers and sisters, whenever you face trials of any kind, consider it nothing but joy, because you know that the testing of your faith produces endurance; and let endurance have its full effect, so that you may be mature and complete, lacking in nothing. (James 1:2–4).

Compare this to Paul's writing in Romans:

We boast in our sufferings, knowing that suffering produces endurance, and endurance produces character, and character produces hope, and hope does not disappoint us, because God's love has been poured into our hearts through the Holy Spirit that has been given to us. (Rom. 5:3–4)

Both Paul and James believe in the character-building nature of suffering, and that the endurance of persecution produces hope and joy. James's use of Paul's language is a hint that he has Paul's letter in mind even as he writes his own.

James also visits a favorite topic of Paul's: boasting. "Let the believer who is lowly boast in being raised up, and the rich in being brought low, because the rich will disappear like a flower in the field" (1:9–10). Both James and Paul likely have in mind Jeremiah 9:24, which tells people not to boast in wealth or in might, but in the Lord. Paul likewise tells Jews not to boast of their special relationship to God (Rom. 2:17).

James moves toward a topic which characterizes the rest of his letter.

But be doers of the word, and not merely hearers who deceive themselves. For if any are hearers of the word and not doers, they are like those who look at themselves in a mirror; for they look at themselves and, on going away, immediately forget what they were like. But those who look into the perfect law, the law of liberty, and persevere, being not hearers who forget but doers who act—they will be blessed in their doing. (James 1:22–25)

Like Paul, James seems to believe that there is a law greater than the Law of Moses, what Paul calls the "law of the Spirit of life" (Rom. 8:1–2), and which James calls the "law of liberty" (James 1:25). I believe that James and Paul have the same idea in mind. The law of liberty is the law that is written on the hearts of people regardless of their culture or religion, the law that allows a devout Muslim, a devout Christian, a devout Jew, and a devout Hindu to recognize each other as kindred spirits because they love both God and neighbor. It is the law that leads a Samaritan to help a wounded man on the side of a road, or a Roman centurion to recognize that Jesus Christ is truly the Son of God. It is the law that is written on the heart of a young woman who, upon hearing a Christian preacher condemn her gay friends as hell-bound abominations, recognizes that his words do not sound much like Jesus, and decides to leave a bigoted church.

James makes a distinction between those who hear only, and those who do. Again, he echoes Paul's letter to the Romans: "It is not the hearers of the law who are righteous in God's sight, but the doers of the law who will be justified" (Rom. 2:13). Both argue that actions demonstrate the law that is written upon the hearts of believers. Those who do good show the law is written on their hearts. Those who do evil show that it is not. There is, in other words, an ethical component to faith. Our actions reveal how true our belief is. James gives three examples of how we express this belief: in how we act (1:25), how we speak (1:26), and our relation to the poor (1:27).

Which brings James to one of his pet peeves: partiality. This particular kind of partiality expresses itself not as Jew versus Gentile, or male versus female, but as rich versus poor. It is class division:

> My brothers and sisters, do you with your acts of favoritism really believe in our glorious Lord Jesus Christ? For if a person with gold rings and in fine clothes comes into your assembly, and if a poor person in dirty clothes also comes in, and if you take notice of the one wearing the fine clothes and say, "Have a seat here, please," while to the one who is poor you say, "Stand there," or, "Sit at my feet," have you not made distinctions among yourselves, and become judges with evil thoughts? (James 2:1–4)

Whether James has a particular episode or recurring problem in mind, or whether he intends this as a hypothetical illustration, it is clear that he believes members are in danger of importing the class divisions of their society into the church. In contrast to the unified, egalitarian picture of church life Luke draws for us in Acts, where believers sell their possessions and share everything in common (Acts 4:32–35), James sees a stratified church in which status and honor is determined by income.

Honor was a form of currency in the cultures of the ancient near east. Benefactors would have no problem contributing funds to build a fountain or forum for a city if it included a flattering statue of themselves. This kind of behavior was not considered self-aggrandizing or crass. Honor and status greased the wheels of politics and the economy. Everyone knew that it was important to sit at important places at the table, eat with the right people, and go to the right social functions. Those who had honor had political cachet. They could call in favors. Their emissaries or disciples would be respected.

Jesus himself apparently had tremendous honor. When he sent out his disciples (Luke 10:1–7) he had little fear that people would not welcome, house, feed, and respect them. People wanted this traveling rabbi as a guest of honor at their table (Luke 11:37), and his choice of dinner host conferred honor to that household. When Jesus chose Zacchaeus to host him, people grumbled because Jesus chose to confer honor on a tax collector, a Judean who collaborated with Rome to defraud his neighbors (Luke 19:5–8). Jesus had a reputation for breaking the honor protocol. The gospel of John says that at the last supper, Jesus even took the role of a slave, washing the feet of his own disciples (John 13:3–11).

Hearing this letter as if it were written to modern American churches doesn't take much of a stretch. Churches remain heavily segregated by both race and class. Three hundred years ago, John Wesley lamented the fact that as his new converts joined class meetings and became spiritually disciplined, they became so prosperous that they forgot to be charitable to the poor:

> For wherever true Christianity spreads, it must cause diligence and frugality, which, in the natural course of things, must beget riches! And riches naturally beget pride, love of the world, and every temper that is destructive of Christianity.[54]

A church that did not give generously to the poor was in danger of losing the power of godliness, he said, while retaining the form. One of Wesley's rules was that people were not allowed to rent prominent pews in worship. Seating was to be general admission-only. There would be no privileged worshipers.

---

54   John Wesley, "Sermon 116: Causes of the Inefficacy of Christianity," Global Ministries, 2011, http://new.gbgm-umc.org/umhistory/wesley/sermons/116.

It is a truism that the most segregated hour of the week in America is still Sunday worship. Fifty years after the civil rights movement, churches are still segregated by race. Even though children attend public school with people of diverse backgrounds and adults work in multiethnic offices and factories, when they come to church they worship where people are mostly homogenous. Our secular culture is more integrated than our religious culture.

Classism and racism are not the only ways we discriminate. While we moderns find the honor/shame system of the ancient world comically self-important, we still have ways of communicating our statuses and claiming our identities in elite social groups. One way of doing this is not through what we wear (though dress does communicate messages about class), but through geography. We may not put sculptures of ourselves up in public venues or strive for the best seats at the table, but we don't need to. Our status is determined by our neighborhood, our school system, and where we shop.

When I've taken groups of people on international mission trips, Americans often see sharp class distinctions side-by-side for the first time. A woman selling cigarettes to passersby shouts at a businessman in a three-piece suit. Office buildings loom over hustlers trying to scrape together enough money to live. Opulent homes with three-car garages sit next to rusting metal-roofed hovels. We don't see these distinctions in our suburbs because we choose not to. Rich and poor in most of our communities don't live anywhere near each other. If they do, the distinctions are purposely hidden. Rich churches and poor churches occupy different parts of town.

James believes that since Jesus had demonstrated radical impartiality in his own life, his followers should likewise reject, or at least suspend, the social hierarchy of the honor/shame system in their worship. James is appalled that they do not live up to this ideal, and again he sounds like someone who has Paul's letter to the Romans in mind:

You do well if you really fulfill the royal law according to the scripture, "You shall love your neighbor as yourself." But if you show partiality, you commit sin and are convicted by the law as transgressors. For whoever keeps the whole law but fails in one point has become accountable for all of it. (James 2:8–10)

Like Paul, James argues that failing in one part of the law means that we are guilty of breaking all of it. He says that partiality is a sin. Those who make distinctions between the rich and poor in their worship have broken the law of loving their neighbor as themselves. By this logic, they are as much transgressors of the law as one who commits adultery or murder. James seems to be aware of the potential this principle has for being abused. He does not want the church to become sin police, so he goes on to invoke the law of liberty again, saying that everyone should therefore "speak and act as those who are to be judged by the law of liberty" (2:12). Both Paul and James want their congregations to be impartial, and to extend grace to each other instead of judging each other: "For judgment will be without mercy to anyone who has shown no mercy; mercy triumphs over judgment" (2:13).

James then begins his famous faith-without-works-is-dead passage:

What good is it, my brothers and sisters, if you say you have faith but do not have works? Can faith save you? If a brother or sister is naked and lacks daily food, and one of you says to them, "Go in peace; keep warm and eat your fill," and yet you do not supply their bodily needs, what is the good of that? So faith by itself, if it has no works, is dead. (James 2:14-17)

James's illustration highlights a theological point that many modern Christians overlook. It is not saying "God bless you" to hungry brothers or sisters that keeps them from starving—it is food. God's action in saving humanity is like giving a hungry person food: a behavior, James suggests, we should emulate. God's salvation comes not from pie-in-the-sky clichés and lofty theological ideas. It comes in the form of bread. Housing. Justice.

We can surmise from James's writing that Paul's argument that "we are saved by faith and not by works" has already been appropriated and misinterpreted by the church as an excuse for turning its back on the poor.

Instead of thinking of "works of the law" the way Paul meant it, as circumcision and dietary regulations, people began thinking of the whole law and what it represented. Some of the most important commandments of God in the Hebrew Bible became irrelevant to them. Some of those laws included loving our neighbors as ourselves, loving the aliens among us, and giving animals and servants a rest on the Sabbath instead of working them to death. If we cannot "earn" our way into heaven by doing them, why bother? All we need are the right beliefs and doctrines about Jesus.

This is the same interpretation I referred to in the dialogue that began this chapter. Too many Christians believe that the Good News is not that the poor and the outcast are welcome at God's table, not that so-called "sinners" and so-called "religious folks" are equally in need and equally receive God's grace, not that God has blessed the world with a glimpse of the kingdom in the self-giving life of Jesus and the church, but that God will let you in to heaven when you die if you accept Jesus. This kind of religion has put believing the right things ahead of doing the right things, and separated the inward life from its outward expression.

James, still referencing Paul, also turns to the example of Abraham. James uses the *exact same scripture* that Paul uses from Genesis 15:6, but gives it a different twist:

> Was not our ancestor Abraham justified by works when he offered his son Isaac on the altar? You see that faith was active along with his works, and faith was brought to completion by the works. Thus the scripture was fulfilled that says, "Abraham believed God, and it was reckoned to him as righteousness," and he was called the friend of God. You see that a person is justified by works and not by faith alone. (James 2:21–24)

Using the same story Paul uses, James points his hearers in a different direction. It was not merely faith, but *faith in action* that justified Abraham. It was not simply the fact that Abraham believed God, but that he believed him strongly enough to risk his only son that demonstrated his faith.

Again, hear this passage not as a philosophical treatise, but as a letter or a word of advice to Christian churches. Rather than thinking about "faith" and "works" as abstract principles, hear how James wants churches to behave. After listening to church members quote Paul and use the story of Abraham to rationalize their inaction, James uses the same story to remind them that action is important. To Christians who are reluctant to part with their money to help the poor, James tells the story of Abraham, who was willing to part with his son. James has taken the misappropriated rhetoric of Paul and turned it back upon those who use it as an excuse for inaction.

James wants to motivate people to act. Right belief is not enough, he argues. "You believe that God is one; you do well," he says. "Even the demons believe—and shudder (2:19)!" You can hear the sarcasm behind his words. "Oh, well done!" we can hear him say. "Even the devils know Jesus is Lord!"

Confessing Jesus as Lord means, though, that Jesus is the God who shows no partiality. This Jesus was an itinerant rabbi who drank a little too much (Matt. 11:19), relativized food regulations (Mark 7:19), failed to ceremonially wash his hands before eating (Mark 7:3), and ate with sinners and tax collectors. He died on a cross rather than bring the wrath of Rome (not to mention the wrath of God) down on the people who wanted to make him king, and in his resurrection demonstrated the power of God to defeat death. If we declare *this* Jesus as Lord, we claim as our king a God who shows no partiality, who welcomes prodigal sons and elder sons alike to the banquet in the coming kingdom. When we declare *this* Jesus as Lord we are not merely pledging allegiance to a particular creed—we are saying something about the character of God. If *Jesus* is Lord (and not Caesar), if *Jesus* is the Son of God (and not Caesar), then there is nothing this old world can do to separate us from the love of God. We cannot be enslaved by social status, or poverty, or accident of birth, or nationality, or ethnicity, or any other human-made division that blocks people from coming to the table.

So the very argument of whether faith or works saves us, or whether one requires the other, misses the point of *both* Paul's *and* James's writing. Both Paul and James agree that the God at work in the saving action of Jesus Christ is the God who shows no partiality between rich and poor or Jews and Gentiles. Both reference Abraham as an example of righteousness who lived at least five hundred years before the Law of Moses. They both write to conflicted communities in which people show partiality toward one group or another, and both, with stinging rhetoric, argue that this kind of partiality calls into question a Christian's commitment to Jesus.

Both Paul and James challenge the church—that's us—to live as though we really have faith that God is at work in Christ, and that grace is sufficient to bring people into the kingdom of God. We overcome our own partiality by living as though we have faith that Jesus is truly Lord, and that he is the God who shows no partiality.

CHAPTER 5:

JESUS'S IMPARTIALITY

Teacher, we know that you are sincere, and show deference to no one; for
you do not regard people with partiality, but teach the way of God in accordance with truth.

Mark 12:13

The Good _____

The guest teacher at the church conference had wrapped up her presenta-
tion, and asked for questions. A hand shot up from a man on the front row.
She raised her eyebrows at him, and he spoke.

"So, I believe I understand what you are saying, but can you boil it
down for me? What is the most important thing I should take away from
the Bible?"

She shrugged, "You know it as well as I do. Love God and love your
neighbor."

He persisted. "But hang on just a minute. Lots of things get excused in
the name of love. How does God *really* want us to behave?"

"Maybe you've heard this story," she said. "Two thugs attacked a man
on a city street and left him to die. Luckily, a Roman Catholic priest saw
the whole thing from a restaurant window. Now, the priest had grown up
in the church. He had read that Jesus identifies with the poor, the sick, and
the wounded. He knew that Jesus said, 'As you have done it to the least of
these, you have done it to me.'[55] He was so disturbed by what he saw that
he got his check, paid his bill, and left. It was a dangerous part of town."

---

55   Matthew 25:40

The audience chuckled.

"A mainline Protestant Christian pulled up at the traffic light and saw the man. He looked carefully at the human being lying in the gutter, and thought about doing something. He even daydreamed a little bit about being the hero. He also considered the possibility that the beaten man was just a drunk, and probably slept on the street. Then the light changed, and he was already late, so he drove on."

"I know this story," said the man in the front row.

"No, you don't," the teacher replied. "Because the next person who came along was a Muslim. He pulled up to the curb and bundled the man into his car, disregarding the blood oozing onto his back seat. He drove the man to the hospital.

"So, to answer your question, How should we show love to others? Maybe we should try to be more like an exemplary Muslim."

The man glared at her. When the evening ended, the audience gave her lukewarm applause.

Gospels with an Agenda

We've seen how food regulations, circumcision, gender, and class all created problems for the early church. If we accept that "God shows no partiality" was a slogan of this early church, we can begin to see how that slogan influenced the writing of the gospels. We can hear echoes of lingering church resentment over theological fights, regrets about missed opportunities, and nostalgia for the "early days." Sayings of Jesus like, "The Sabbath was made for humankind, not humankind for the Sabbath," or, "Things that go into us don't make us unclean; words and actions that come out of us do," were clearly meant to reinforce the principle of God's impartiality. Many of these Jesus quotations sound like slogans and rhetorical arguments made by the early church for the full inclusion of Gentiles, and they give us a model for how to live in a religiously pluralistic world.

The four gospels, Matthew, Mark, Luke, and John, were all written well after Jesus lived and walked among his disciples. The general consensus of biblical scholars is that the author of Mark wrote his gospel around 50 to 60 CE, around thirty or forty years after Jesus. Matthew and Luke-

Acts were most likely written after the destruction of Jerusalem by the Roman army in 70 CE. The gospel of John was the latest, between 100 and 110, nearly seventy years after Jesus. There was plenty of time for the early church to reflect upon and interpret what God was continuing to do in their communities.

It is unlikely that Jesus's disciples followed him around with a notepad and pen, recording everything he said. The sayings and stories of Jesus were handed down as oral tradition. Scholars theorize that Matthew and Luke may have had access to an early written collection of sayings, which they call "Q."[56] These are Jesus sound bites, bits of wisdom and parables collected from here and there. This means that the authors of the gospels relied on communal memory and their own imaginations to plug these sayings into a context. So when the gospel authors tell stories of Jesus, they don't tell every single thing Jesus ever did. They tell only certain Jesus stories. After all, a year or three of ministry cannot be condensed into a gospel you can read in one sitting.

We do the same thing even with recent historical events and people. There are many quotations and stories attributed to Winston Churchill, Mark Twain, and Alfred Hitchcock that may or may not be completely accurate, but all of them reflect our cultural appreciation of them as quick-witted, funny, and wise. We do not tell stories about the day Mark Twain did the laundry, or the time Winston Churchill failed to make a witty reply to an insult.

So, when we read about a woman sitting at Jesus's feet as if she had the same status as a male disciple (Luke 10:39), or about Jesus telling a story about a Samaritan woman (John 4), we are reading stories that the authors choose to tell their communities for a reason. They want their readers and hearers to experience a particular side of Jesus and to understand Jesus in a certain light. In other words, they have an agenda. Because the early church was shaped by debates with *Christian* Pharisees over how closely members

---

56   From the German quelle, which means "source." This is a hypothetical document that may have resembled other extant collections of Jesus's sayings. See "Sayings Gospels," in *The Complete Gospels*, ed. Robert J. Miller (Santa Rosa: Polebridge Press, 1994).

of the new community would follow the Law of Moses, the gospels consistently place the *non-Christian* Pharisees on the wrong side of arguments with Jesus. I'm not asserting that these arguments never happened, but that the authors are particularly interested in these debates because they want to highlight the principle of Jesus's impartiality.

It may help to read of the gospels as you would read the editorial page of a newspaper. A common way for these kinds of writers to address a problem is to talk about how it was addressed in history. For example, a writer may tell a story about his Irish immigrant ancestor and the prejudice he faced as he made a new life in America over a hundred years ago. He writes not just to tell his readers interesting facts about history, but to share his opinion on how our communities should treat Latino immigrants today. In the same way, the gospel authors tell stories of Jesus's encounters with the Pharisees not merely to share interesting history, but to shape how the early church thought about the inclusion of Gentiles and the factions that would exclude them.[57]

Pharisees and Jesus

In speaking about Jesus and the Pharisees, it's important to remember that they were part of the same group. While Jesus had particular positions on theological arguments that arose among the Pharisees, he engaged them as one of their own number, and not as an outsider.

The Pharisees were champions of the belief that the priests had done a poor job of educating Israelites about holiness. In contrast to the priesthood, the Pharisees were a lay movement that emphasized that Israel should be a holy nation, and that holiness was not just for priests but for everyone. Everyone (who had the spare time) could read the Torah and learn about what God wanted from their lives. Temple observance was only one aspect of a vision God had for the world. The other aspect was ethics, and the Pharisees were the people to teach everyone about it.

The prophet Malachi summed up their gripes about the Temple priests. Malachi lived about four hundred years before Jesus, and had spoken harsh words to the priests of his day when he compared them to an ideal teacher:

---

57   I am doing the same thing with the words you are reading now.

True instruction was in his mouth, and no wrong was found on his lips. He walked with me in integrity and uprightness, and he turned many from iniquity. For the lips of a priest should guard knowledge, and people should seek instruction from his mouth, for he is the messenger of the Lord of hosts. But you have turned aside from the way; you have caused many to stumble by your instruction; you have corrupted the covenant of Levi, says the Lord of hosts, and so I make you despised and abased before all the people, inasmuch as you have not kept my ways but have shown partiality in your instruction. (Mal. 2:6–9)

The Pharisees believed in what Malachi said, and this particular group recognized in Jesus this same philosophy. Therefore when they approach Jesus with a question about paying taxes to the emperor, they compare him to the ideal teacher in Malachi. They are the only ones to actually call Jesus impartial in the New Testament:

Then they sent to him some Pharisees and some Herodians to trap him in what he said. And they came and said to him, "Teacher, we know that you are sincere, and show deference to no one; for you do not regard people with partiality, but teach the way of God in accordance with truth. Is it lawful to pay taxes to the emperor, or not? Should we pay them, or should we not?" But knowing their hypocrisy, he said to them, "Why are you putting me to the test? Bring me a denarius and let me see it." And they brought one. Then he said to them, "Whose head is this, and whose title?" They answered, "The emperor's." Jesus said to them, "Give to the emperor the things that are the emperor's, and to God the things that are God's." And they were utterly amazed at him. (Mark 12:13–17)

With the church disputes over circumcision and food regulations fresh in his mind, Mark may savor the delicious irony of the Pharisees espousing the principle of impartiality. He makes them sound particularly sarcastic, as though they were saying "Hey, there, college boy. You're such a brainiac.

Answer us this..." As early Christian communities retold this story, they may have chuckled since, for them, Jesus *was* the good teacher who taught the true way of God and did not regard people with partiality. The Pharisees intend the phrase sarcastically, but it is more true than they realize. Mark also adds an editorial comment: Jesus *knows* their hypocrisy. They are wearing masks, but Jesus recognizes that they are play-actors.

After silencing the Pharisees, Jesus turns to the crowds. He publicly ridicules the Pharisees, excoriating them for their hypocrisy. His rant lasts an entire chapter in Matthew's gospel. When Jesus begins his diatribe, we can hear in his angry words more echoes of the conflicts over circumcision and food regulations in the early church.

> [The Pharisees] tie up heavy burdens, hard to bear, and lay them on the shoulders of others; but they themselves are unwilling to lift a finger to move them. (Matt. 23:4)

His words here sound remarkably like Peter's speech in Acts, when he says that circumcision is "a yoke neither our ancestors nor we have been able to bear" (Acts 15:10). Jesus continues:

> They do all their deeds to be seen by others; for they make their phylacteries broad and their fringes long. They love to have the place of honor at banquets and the best seats in the synagogues, and to be greeted with respect in the marketplaces, and to have people call them rabbi.

> But you are not to be called rabbi, for you have one teacher, and you are all students. And call no one your father on earth, for you have one Father—the one in heaven. Nor are you to be called instructors, for you have one instructor, the Messiah. The greatest among you will be your servant. All who exalt themselves will be humbled, and all who humble themselves will be exalted. (Matt. 23:5–12)

For Matthew's Jesus, the ideal church is egalitarian.[58] God's impartiality means members have a radical new way of relating to each other. They will have no officers: teachers, fathers, reverends, or any other. The criteria for greatness in the new community is not knowledge or seniority, but humility and love. Divine impartiality means that hierarchies in the church get flattened. Nobody gets to act greater than anyone else.

By contrast, the Pharisees are Matthew's mirror image of the church: hierarchical, judgmental, and partial:

> But woe to you, scribes and Pharisees, hypocrites! For you lock people out of the kingdom of heaven. For you do not go in yourselves, and when others are going in, you stop them. Woe to you, scribes and Pharisees, hypocrites! For you cross sea and land to make a single convert, and you make the new convert twice as much a child of hell as yourselves. (Matt. 23:13–15)

I would never argue that Jesus *didn't* say these words, but I think it's safe to say that in Matthew's Jesus we hear the author's own lingering resentment over past church conflicts.

Matthew's Jesus also warns the church not to judge the Christianity of other Christians. Only Jesus, the impartial judge, has the authority to do that at the end of the age (Matt. 13:39). Nor does length of service give some people more authority in the church than others. In the parable of the workers in the vineyard (20:1–16), the newbies get the same reward as the old-timers. No person in Matthew's church is privileged over any other. God's impartiality should be reflected in the church's life together.

We've already examined some of the other features of this egalitarian church. For Matthew, the new community of impartiality stands in contrast to the old one not only because there are no more ranks and status symbols, but also because it includes Gentiles and God-fearing Romans like Cornelius. In Matthew 8:5–13, another centurion approaches Jesus and

---

58   See Edgar Krentz, "Egalitarian Church of Matthew," *Currents in Theology and Mission* 4, no. 6 (1977).

asks him to heal the centurion's servant. Jesus makes ready to go, but the centurion says, "Wait, just heal him from here." Jesus responds, "Truly I tell you, in no one in Israel have I found such faith" (Matt. 8:10). The centurion even calls Jesus "Lord," which was treasonous language for someone whose primary allegiance was due to Caesar.

This anonymous centurion and Cornelius are two of three Roman military commanders in the New Testament who show faith in Jesus. The third is present at the crucifixion and claims that Jesus was the son of God and innocent of any crime (Mark 15:39; Matt. 28:54; Luke 23:47). Including these characters in the gospels was a way of telling early Gentile Christians that there was no animosity toward Romans on the part of the church. Portraying Roman centurions in the story of Jesus's ministry and in the life of the early church is a gesture of radical inclusivity.

Although the Jews were the covenant people, Jesus indicates that all kinds of people can now claim part of the covenant; not only Romans and those of other nations, but even those who have lapsed religiously:

> "What do you think? A man had two sons; he went to the first and said, 'Son, go and work in the vineyard today.' He answered, 'I will not'; but later he changed his mind and went. The father went to the second and said the same; and he answered, 'I go, sir'; but he did not go. Which of the two did the will of his father?" They said, "The first." Jesus said to them, "Truly I tell you, the tax-collectors and the prostitutes are going into the kingdom of God ahead of you. For John came to you in the way of righteousness and you did not believe him, but the tax-collectors and the prostitutes believed him; and even after you saw it, you did not change your minds and believe him." (Matt. 21:28–32)

There are, Jesus says, not only religious insiders who avoid God's work, but also unreligious outsiders who do God's work (like the Good Samaritan).

Modern Christians often use the phrase "tax collectors and prostitutes" in church, but it has little shock value because we are not familiar with the process of tax farming and temple prostitution. A tax collector was not an IRS agent, and a prostitute was not simply a street-walker. Tax collectors, or tax farmers, made bids on how much money they could extract from a local population. Their job required them to be intimately familiar with their neighbors' business. To their own people, they were traitors who colluded with the Roman occupiers. Prostitutes, whether they served in a temple cult or simply freelanced, were everything the prophets of the Hebrew Bible had railed against. Temple prostitutes represented the pagan religions that lured Israel away from the worship of YHWH. The people had "played the whore" (Hosea 4:15) by visiting temple prostitutes. Prostitutes were responsible for the moral and spiritual decay of the nation. Tax collectors and prostitutes stood for everything that destroyed the ancient nations of Israel and Judah, and were opposed to everything the homeland represented in the national and religious consciousness of the Jews.

We would need to think of other kinds of people who represent predatory moneymaking and moral decay: extortionists and hookers, casino owners and porn stars, hedge-fund investors and reality-television celebrities. Yet Jesus says that people of this sort who secretly do good are more righteous than preachers and religious leaders who say a lot of good things but avoid God's work. It's a scandalous assertion that the modern church has to learn again and again.

In the early church's memory of Jesus, his friendliness with tax collectors and prostitutes is simply another example of divine impartiality, which the Pharisees oppose. When Jesus eats with tax collectors and sinners, the Pharisees grumble to the disciples, "Why does he eat with such riff-raff?" (Mark 2:16, Matt. 9:11). When Jesus compares his ministry with the teetotaler John the Baptist, he says

John came neither eating nor drinking, and they say, "He has a demon"; the Son of Man came eating and drinking, and they say, "Look, a glutton and a drunkard, a friend of tax-collectors and sinners!" Yet wisdom is vindicated by her deeds. (Matt. 11:18–19).

Whether or not Jesus actually does eat and drink too much is less important than the fact that his reputation as a glutton and drunkard is enhanced by the company he keeps. Someone who eats with these kinds of people, enjoying feasts paid for with their ill-gotten wealth, *must* be a drunkard and a glutton.[59]

Not all the Pharisees rejected Jesus. There were obviously Pharisees who supported him. Part of the reason Jesus spends so much time with Pharisees is that he is very much like them. Jesus goes to the synagogue on the Sabbath, wears the fringed shawl of someone who follows the Law of Moses (Matt. 9:20), emphasizes ethical behavior as a way of obeying God, argues scripture like a Pharisee, quotes prominent Pharisees of his day, and has Pharisee followers and friends like Joseph of Arimathea (Luke 23:50), Nicodemus (John 3), and Simon (Luke 7:36). On one occasion Pharisees act to save him from Herod (Luke 13:31), and more than once he eats with prominent Pharisees (Luke 7; 11:37; 14). Occasionally scribes also win Jesus's approval (Mark 12:28–34). So while these religious leaders take the brunt of Jesus's criticism in the gospels, it's important to recognize that they played an important role in his ministry. Modern scholars recognize that when Jesus speaks against the Pharisees, he does so as a member of their own group, critiquing it from within. It would be like a Methodist preacher saying from the pulpit, "The problem with Methodists is…"

Sloganeering

Sayings of Jesus like, "The Sabbath was made for humankind, not humankind for the Sabbath," or, "Things that go into us don't make us unclean; words and actions that come out of us do," were clearly meant to reinforce the principle of God's impartiality. Some of these Jesus quotations were slogans and rhetorical arguments made by the early church for the full inclusion of Gentiles.

According to the gospels, Jesus constantly provokes the Pharisees with opportunities to show their partiality. Jesus violates the Sabbath by allowing his disciples to pluck grain (Matt. 12:1–8), healing a man with a with-

---

59   The modern church retains some of this memory in the language of the Lord's Supper. The liturgy shared by most mainline and Catholic churches says that Jesus "healed the sick, fed the hungry, and ate with sinners." *The United Methodist Hymnal* (Nashville, TN: The United Methodist Publishing House, 1989), 10.

ered hand (Matt. 12:9–14),[60] and healing a lame man in Jerusalem (John 5). The Pharisees go apoplectic, and begin to conspire "how to destroy him."

Again, most Christians take these stories at face value, and in thousands of sermons in churches all over the world the Pharisees come off as being overly concerned with minor infractions. But Jesus is being deliberately provocative. When his disciples pluck and eat raw grains of wheat on the Sabbath, it is like making a meal out of a handful of sunflower seeds. This is why the Law of Moses (Deut. 23:25) allows travelers to pluck a few heads from someone else's field. It will hardly hurt the final harvest, and is not so much an act of stealing on the part of the traveler as an act of hospitality on the part of the owner. But if it's such a minor thing, then how necessary is it for the disciples to do this kind of work? Since they are so small, Matthew seems to argue, the Pharisees shouldn't make a big deal of them. But the Pharisees could just as easily argue that since the grains are so small, the disciples don't need to pick them. Jesus allows the whole episode to happen in order to make a point about his identity: he is greater than the Sabbath (and the Temple, he adds, as though to provoke more anger).

Nor does Jesus need to heal any particular person on the Sabbath. In one story, he heals a man with a withered hand, which outrages the Pharisees (Matthew 12:9-14). Jesus compares the situation to helping a sheep that falls into a pit, but a withered hand is not a life-threatening problem.[61] It is a chronic condition which the man has been living with for years. In our own society, if a man with such a condition tried to see a doctor on a Sunday, he'd be told to come back during office hours on Monday. Jesus does not *have* to heal the man on the Sabbath, any more than the disciples *have* to eat heads of grain. He does these things so he can say, "The Sabbath was made for humankind, and not humankind for the Sabbath" (Mark 2:27).

It's easy to imagine either of these Sabbath slogans in the mouth of a Christian laborer in the early church. If he worked for a non-Jewish boss, he might not be able to take Saturday off. Other church members might

---

60   See also Luke 6 and Mark 2:23–3:6
61   Luke tells a similar story about a crippled woman (Luke 13:10–17). Jesus is more eloquent in Luke's story, describing healing as a kind of liberation, which is totally appropriate for Sabbath work.

encourage him to resist the way Daniel or Eleazar did under their persecution. But Jesus gives him another option: he can follow the example of Jesus in these stories. The worker does not have to force a confrontation with his boss. After all, "The Sabbath was made for humankind, and not humankind for the Sabbath." Jesus himself had demonstrated it. So by relaxing Sabbath rules, the church opened itself up to people with different working situations.

The Pharisees wind up on the wrong side of the argument again when they observe that some of Jesus's disciples don't wash their hands when they eat (Mark 7:1–23). Washing hands before meals was not about hygiene, as it is for modern people. People of Jesus's day were not aware of bacteria or viruses as agents of disease. Religious people washed their hands to be ritually clean. It has more in common with the way modern Christians might pray or "say grace" before eating. As a pastor, I'm often called on to thank God for our food at a public meal. More than once I've been at restaurants with groups of people from different faith backgrounds, and rather than assume everyone is a Christian who wants to pray before eating, I simply tucked in while the Christians in the group sat awkwardly or stared at me in disapproval. This is apparently the same kind of awkward situation Jesus created by not washing his hands before eating. People looked at him and his disciples and silently judged their lack of religious propriety.

Jesus points out the problem with this kind of thinking, and expands it to cover all the food regulations of the Law of Moses. "Listen to me, all of you, and understand," he calls out to the crowd. "There is nothing outside a person that by going in can defile, but the things that come out are what defile" (Mark 7:14-16). Later, in private, he repeats himself and adds the scatological element, telling the disciples that food "enters not the heart, but the stomach, and passes out into the sewer" (Mark 7:19). Just in case his audience may miss the broader point he wants to make, Mark adds the parenthetical comment, "Thus [Jesus] declared all foods clean."

We've already imagined the impact of this statement from the Pharisees' point of view, and of the scandal it must have caused. Now imagine the impact this saying might have had for a Gentile in Corinth. When Gentile Christians who believed it was okay to eat idol-sacrificed meat confronted their opponents, they could respond, "Food enters not the heart, but the stomach, and goes out into the sewer." The Pharisees and abstaining Christians thus wind up on the wrong side of Jesus. Thinking they were the in-group, they are revealed by his clever rhetoric to be the out-group. It isn't the mask we wear or the food choices we make that matter to God. It is the content of our character. "It is what comes out of a person that defiles"—fornication, avarice, slander, and so on—all of which are much nastier than excrement.

These kinds of stories about conflicts with Pharisees are chock-full of Jesus quotes that could become handy slogans in the mouths of Christians who argued for the full inclusion of Gentiles. They were meant to display something of the character of the impartial Jesus. They also worked like rhetorical crowbars: they gave Christians the tools to dismantle discrimination in the church based on religious regulations or spiritual superiority. We've inherited their legacy. Any time anyone claims to be "more Christian" than someone else, we should become suspicious of their motivations.

Who Is the Greatest?

Although the gospel authors heap scorn on the Pharisees for their failure to grasp the principle of impartiality, they have their share for the disciples as well. Mark, in particular, is known for portraying the disciples as numbskulls. Not only do they fail to recognize Jesus as Lord and Messiah, they do not immediately understand that the principle of impartiality should characterize their life together. They argue over who is the greatest (Mark 9:33), and jockey for position over who will get to sit at Jesus's right hand when he is crowned king over the new kingdom (Mark 10:37). Jesus informs them that

> whoever wishes to become great among you must be your servant, and whoever wishes to be first among you must be slave of all. For the Son of Man came not to be served but to serve, and to give his life a ransom for many. (Mark 10:43–45).

This is an example of a situation in which the principle of God's impartiality inverts the status quo. It says that not only does God disregard the social status of people, but that God actually honors those with lower status *more*. Impartiality does not mean that everyone is equal. In fact, in the topsy-turvy kingdom of God, status and greatness will be reversed. When Jesus sees people scrambling for the best seats at a banquet, he admonishes them, "All who exalt themselves will be humbled, and those who humble themselves will be exalted" (Luke 14:11).

Another example of God's privileging of those without status is when Jesus blesses children.

> People were bringing little children to him in order that he might touch them; and the disciples spoke sternly to them. But when Jesus saw this, he was indignant and said to them, "Let the little children come to me; do not stop them; for it is to such as these that the kingdom of God belongs. Truly I tell you, whoever does not receive the kingdom of God as a little child will never enter it." And he took them up in his arms, laid his hands on them, and blessed them. (Mark 10:13–16)

Bill Gandy, one of my preacher friends, pointed out in a baptismal sermon that this is the only time in the New Testament that Jesus is described as being "indignant." "Irate" may be a better translation. "Can you imagine the look on Jesus's face?" asked Bill. "Would you want to be on that side of Jesus?" After Jesus rebukes the disciples for excluding children, he not only touches them, but he also picks them up in his arms, lays hands on them, and blesses them.

Modern people find nothing unusual with this extravagant attention paid to children, but until relatively recently in Western civilization, children were seen and not heard. The great shift in our attitudes toward children began in the industrial revolution. Before Charles Dickens's stories about Oliver Twist or David Copperfield, before Sigmund Freud and developmental psychology, before mandatory public schooling, you'd be hard-pressed to find much written about childhood that didn't see it as something to be escaped and left behind as soon as possible. There were no wistful or romantic notions about "growing up too fast." To be called "child-like" would never be a compliment. It would be an insult. When Paul talks about spiritual enlightenment, he talks about becoming a man and putting away childish ways (1 Cor. 13:11).[62] While it was a blessing to have children, and a sign of God's favor to have many children, children themselves were nobodies. When Jesus says that the kingdom of God belong to "such as these," he is saying that the kingdom of God belongs to nobodies.[63]

It is possible to read this story other ways. Children were not required to follow the Law of Moses.[64] It may be that to receive the kingdom "as a child" means to receive it as one who is not required to keep the Law—which would include Gentiles. Either way you read it, Jesus is once again illuminating what it means to show no partiality. It is easy to imagine this saying as another slogan in the mouths of early Christians when they argued with old-timer Christians or with those who asserted their spiritual superiority: "Oh yeah?" they might have retorted, "Whoever does not receive the kingdom as a child will never enter it."

Women, Foreigners, and Samaritans

Luke's gospel and his sequel, Acts, are probably the most explicit in their descriptions of an impartial Jesus. Luke's Jesus spends the most time with women, emphasizes most dramatically the upside-down nature of the kingdom of God, and even includes Samaritans among the potentially saved. Luke is where we find the parables of the Good Samaritan (10:25–37) and the Thankful Samaritan (17:11–19), and where he rebukes the disciples for their hostility to Samaritans (9:51–56).[65]

---

62   By implication, Paul belittles anyone who believes that one spiritual gift is better than another.

63   John Dominic Crossan, *The Historical Jesus: The Life of a Mediterranean Jewish Peasant* (San Francisco: Harper, 1991) 269.

64   Judith M. Gundry-Volf, "The Least and the Greatest," in *The Child in Christian Thought*, ed. Marcia J. Bunge (Grand Rapids: Eerdmans, 2001), 39.

65   Mark Allan Powell, *Fortress Introduction to the Gospels* (Minneapolis, MN: Fortress, 1998), 93.

Other gospels also include women in surprising ways: an unnamed woman[66] anoints Jesus at Bethany (Mark 14:3–9); women who financed Jesus's ministry observe his crucifixion while the disciples run and hide (Mark 15:40–41); women are the first to see the risen Lord in all the gospels (Mark 16). Matthew's Jesus also compares God's kingdom to a woman working leaven into a batch of dough (Matt. 13:33).[67] John includes a story about a Samaritan woman who Jesus meets at a well (John 4) and another story about a woman caught in adultery (John 8:1–11).[68]

Luke gives the most voice to women. Both Mary, the mother of Jesus, and her cousin Elizabeth get significant space in Luke's story. Mary breaks into verse in one of the most beautiful poems of the Bible:

My soul magnifies the Lord,
and my spirit rejoices in God my Savior,
for he has looked with favor on the lowliness of his servant.
Surely, from now on all generations will call me blessed;
for the Mighty One has done great things for me,
and holy is his name.
His mercy is for those who fear him
from generation to generation.
He has shown strength with his arm;
he has scattered the proud in the thoughts of their hearts.
He has brought down the powerful from their thrones,
and lifted up the lowly;
he has filled the hungry with good things,
and sent the rich away empty.
He has helped his servant Israel,

---

66 John identifies her with Mary, the sister of Martha (John 12). Luke moves the anointing at Bethany to earlier in Jesus's ministry, and sets up a dialogue about her with a Pharisee named Simon (Luke 7:36)

67 This parable is doubly scandalous. Not only does Jesus compare God to a woman, he compares the kingdom to leaven, something forbidden from holy offerings. David Buttrick, *Speaking Parables* (Louisville: John Knox, 2000), 148.

68 Although they claim she was caught in the act, her accusers conveniently forget to bring along the man for punishment, as well.

in remembrance of his mercy,
according to the promise he made to our ancestors,
to Abraham and to his descendants for ever.
(Luke 1:46–55)

Mary also believes in a God who sees beyond the masks. She evokes God's preferential option for the poor and oppressed. "He has brought down the powerful from their thrones, and lifted up the lowly."

In Luke's gospel, when Jesus launches his ministry, he goes to his boyhood home of Nazareth and attends the synagogue on the Sabbath. The people of his hometown crowd the synagogue, eager to hear what the hometown celebrity has to say. They hand him the scroll and invite him to preach. Like his mother, he chooses a text about God's revolutionary activity on behalf of the poor:

"The Spirit of the Lord is upon me, because he has anointed me to bring good news to the poor. He has sent me to proclaim release to the captives and recovery of sight to the blind, to let the oppressed go free, to proclaim the year of the Lord's favor." And he rolled up the scroll, gave it back to the attendant, and sat down. The eyes of all in the synagogue were fixed on him. Then he began to say to them, "Today this scripture has been fulfilled in your hearing." (Luke 4:18–21)

The congregation approves of his choice of text: "All spoke well of him and were amazed at the gracious words that came from his mouth" (4:22). After all, aren't they oppressed under the boot of Roman occupation? Aren't they kept poor by the ravenous tax collectors? Aren't they captives in their own land? And now Jesus identifies with the prophet in the scripture, and says he will proclaim this good news! The crowd whispers excitedly to themselves: "Is not this Joseph's son?"

The last thing they expect are these words that fall from his mouth:

Truly I tell you, no prophet is accepted in the prophet's home town.
But the truth is, there were many widows in Israel in the time of

Elijah, when the heaven was shut up for three years and six months, and there was a severe famine over all the land; yet Elijah was sent to none of them except to a widow at Zarephath in Sidon. There were also many lepers in Israel in the time of the prophet Elisha, and none of them was cleansed except Naaman the Syrian. (Luke 4:24–27).

Jesus preempts their nationalist pride and prejudice with a stunning retelling of Biblical events. God, he implies, does not privilege Israel. The widows and lepers of Israel are no more favored by God than the widows and lepers of other lands. In the ancient dialogue about what it means to be chosen and unchosen, Jesus comes down squarely in favor of the unchosen.

Their words of admiration turn into shouts of anger. They pick him up and take him to the edge of a cliff, intending to toss him over. Somehow he eludes them and slips through the crowd.

The anger of the citizens of Nazareth have close parallels with Christian prejudices today, because American Christians still assert their moral superiority over other nations and other sinners. In 2010, an earthquake devastated the island nation of Haiti. While most Americans were moved to donate and volunteer their aid for the people of Haiti, one Christian televangelist, Pat Robertson, declared that the disaster was God's judgment upon the people of Haiti for their ancient practice of voodoo.[69] It was not the first time in recent history that a Christian voiced such a reprehensible theology. After the September 11 attacks on the World Trade Center, Jerry Falwell said that God had lifted his protection from America because of the ACLU, pagans, gays, feminists, and lesbians.[70] These leaders always take the opportunity to see disasters as punishment from God when it suits them, but they ignore God's gracious action outside of their own borders or privileged groups.

---

69   Ryan Smith, "Pat Robertson: Haiti 'Cursed' after 'Pact to the Devil,'" CBSNews.com, January 13, 2010, http://www.cbsnews.com/8301-504083_162-12017-504083.html.
70   "Falwell Apologizes to Gays, Feminists, Lesbians," September 14, 2001, CNN, Available: http://articles.cnn.com/2001-09-14/us/Falwell.apology_1_thomas-road-baptist-church-jerry-falwell-feminists?_s=PM:US.

Jesus repudiates this kind of thinking. In another Lukan story, a group of people approach Jesus with a question. Some worshipers from Galilee were killed by Pilate while they were worshiping. Was this a punishment from God? Jesus answers:

> Do you think that because these Galileans suffered in this way they were worse sinners than all other Galileans? No, I tell you; but unless you repent, you will all perish as they did. Or those eighteen who were killed when the tower of Siloam fell on them—do you think that they were worse offenders than all the others living in Jerusalem? No, I tell you; but unless you repent, you will all perish just as they did. (Luke 13:2–5)

Jesus quickly turns the tables on the Jerusalemites who ask him the question. "First of all," he says, "do you think these Galileans were worse than any others? Second of all," he continues, "do you think they were worse than you?" Imagine Jesus saying the same thing to Pat Robertson or Jerry Falwell, and you can hear the anger in his voice. He resents people passing judgment on others because of the bad things that happen to them. The last part of his statement highlights the absurdity of that theology: "unless you repent, the same thing will happen to you." Massacres, falling towers, earthquakes, lightning strikes, and airplane crashes may be what we deserve, but most of us will die by more conventional means.[71]

Jesus goes on to tell a parable.

> A man had a fig tree planted in his vineyard; and he came looking for fruit on it and found none. So he said to the gardener, "See here! For three years I have come looking for fruit on this fig tree, and

71 Another interpretation, of course, is that Luke's listeners would call to mind the destruction of Jerusalem in 70 CE. In this case, Jesus is not repudiating the idea that God gets retribution on people for their sin, but affirming it. I'm not convinced of this for two reasons. First, Jesus's following parable seems to undermine the idea. Second, the rhetoric of Luke's Jesus isn't intended only for Jerusalemites, but for the early church. For them, being killed by persecutors (Acts 7) was not a sign of God's judgment, but God's approval.

still I find none. Cut it down! Why should it be wasting the soil?"
He replied, "Sir, let it alone for one more year, until I dig round it
and put manure on it. If it bears fruit next year, well and good; but
if not, *you* can cut it down." (Luke 13:6–9)

The tree in question has been failing to produce not only for the three
years the owner has come looking for fruit, but the five years required by
the Torah that he is supposed to leave it alone.[72] There is no question that
the tree is a dud. It has been barren for eight years. The gardener, though,
shows an absurd amount of patience. "Let me throw some *kopria* on it,"
he says, "but I won't cut it down. You can do it yourself." Again, just like
he did in Mark 7:19, Jesus uses scatological humor to make his point.
David Buttrick says, "A more earthy word is likely," because the Greek
word "is root for a number of slang terms applied to people—'stinkards,
dirty fellows, low buffoons.'"[73] Whatever word you choose to use, *manure*
is not going to help this tree. The gardener's faith in composted excrement is at best a delay tactic and at worst an offensive refusal. He will
not cut it down.

This parable has often been preached as a story of impending judgment:
the axe is at the root of the tree, and God's wrath is coming. In this interpretation, God is like the landowner who looks only at cost-benefit ratios and
sees no point in keeping around an unproductive plant. But Jesus's point does
not seem to be about God's anger, but about God's ridiculous patience. In
this case, God is more like the gardener, who simply loves growing things. In
light of a God who keeps delaying the rational, obvious, called-for response
to an unfruitful nation, how can we say that a disaster, or a falling tower, or
an earthquake is God's wrath upon sinful people? Just as God "makes his sun
to rise on the evil and on the good, and sends rain on the righteous and on
the unrighteous" (Matt. 5:45), God's impartiality and ridiculously patient
grace mean that God doesn't inflict earthquakes and disasters upon sinners.
Jesus, with a vulgar joke, knocks down the pride of the self-righteously safe.

72 Buttrick, *Speaking Parables*, 194.
73 Buttrick, *Speaking Parables*, 195.

The Samaritans were apparently an easy target for this kind of prejudice. There was bad blood between Samaritans who worshiped God at Mount Gerizim and Jews who worshiped God at the Temple in Jerusalem. The roots of the conflict go back nearly a thousand years before Jesus, when the kingdom of Israel split in two. Judah, the southern kingdom, retained control of the Temple in Jerusalem. Israel, the northern kingdom, established new worship centers to keep its money and people within its own borders. It set up a new capital city named Samaria.

The Judeans believed that the Northern Kingdom (Israel) had not only rejected God's anointed king (David's grandson), but God as well. When the Assyrians destroyed Israel in 721 BCE, the Jerusalemites said that God had destroyed the Northern Kingdom for its apostasy. The conquering Assyrians brought in their own people to repopulate the country. They intermarried with the remnant of the population, took up the worship of Israel's God, and became known as Samaritans, after Israel's capital city.

A little more than a century later, in 587 BCE, the Babylonian Empire swooped in and crushed Judah's capital, Jerusalem, as well. The Samaritans probably felt a sense of poetic justice. The people who had been smug about Israel's downfall had fallen themselves. If God's destruction of Israel was divine punishment for Israel's apostasy, then God's destruction of Jerusalem was divine punishment for Judah's arrogance.

According to the ancient historian Josephus, after the exiles returned to Jerusalem and began rebuilding the temple, the Samaritans approached them and asked to be allowed to help in the reconstruction, since they also worshiped YHWH. The Jerusalemites refused. Since it was clear to the Samaritans that the Jerusalemites had lost none of their exclusivist national pride during exile, the Samaritans tried to stop the building project by writing to the emperor and accusing them of treason, saying that their building was "more like a fortress than a temple." Josephus condemns the Samaritans as being conniving and two-faced.[74] They had even been known to kill Jewish pilgrims to Jerusalem. Their long and complicated history with Jewish worshipers of YHWH meant that among Jesus's people, they

---

74   Josephus, *Antiquities of the Jews* 11.84–97

were treated not as kindred but as foreigners, according to Luke 17:18. It may be more accurate to call them enemies.[75]

But after Jesus, when the early church began to spread into Samaria, it found ready converts even among Samaritans (Acts 8:4-25). Within the early church, then, Jews (including Pharisees) and Samaritans gathered around a common table to declare Jesus as their Lord. Perhaps if modern Christians kept this ancient animosity and reconciliation in mind, sermons about "The Good Samaritan" would sound much different to our ears.

The whole story is told in response to a question. A lawyer asks Jesus, "What must I do to inherit eternal life?" Jesus gets him to answer his own question:

He said to him, "What is written in the law? What do you read there?" He answered, "You shall love the Lord your God with all your heart, and with all your soul, and with all your strength, and with all your mind; and your neighbor as yourself." And he said to him, "You have given the right answer; do this, and you will live." But wanting to justify himself, he asked Jesus, "And who is my neighbor?"

Not content with the usual answer, which everyone with a basic religious education knew (Matt. 19:16–22; 22:34–40), the lawyer tries to get a more detailed answer out of Jesus. What does it actually mean to love your neighbor? In response, Jesus tells a story.

Jesus replied, "A man was going down from Jerusalem to Jericho, and fell into the hands of robbers, who stripped him, beat him, and went away, leaving him half dead. Now by chance a priest was going down that road; and when he saw him, he passed by on the other side. So likewise a Levite, when he came to the place and saw him, passed by on the other side. But a Samaritan while traveling

75 Amy-Jill Levine, "Biblical Views: The Many Faces of the Good Samaritan—Most Wrong." *Biblical Archeology Review*, no. 38:1 January/February 2012, http://www.bibarch.org/bar/article.asp?PubID=BSBA&Volume=38&Issue=01&ArticleID=13.

came near him; and when he saw him, he was moved with pity. He went to him and bandaged his wounds, having poured oil and wine on them. Then he put him on his own animal, brought him to an inn, and took care of him. The next day he took out two denarii, gave them to the innkeeper, and said, 'Take care of him; and when I come back, I will repay you whatever more you spend.' Which of these three, do you think, was a neighbor to the man who fell into the hands of the robbers?" He said, "The one who showed him mercy." Jesus said to him, "Go and do likewise." (Luke 10:26–37)

Most Christians know it's important to help those in need. "Being a Good Samaritan," like having "faith as a child," is something we know we are supposed to do. But Jesus's point is not merely that his listeners should act like the Good Samaritan. The story only works because the lawyer and Jesus's listeners *already know* that it's important to help people in need. The salient point of the story is that the only person who does the right thing is a foreigner.

The lawyer shouldn't be surprised that Jesus uses a foreigner to illustrate love of neighbor, nor should anyone familiar with the Torah. The same chapter that commands followers of God to love their neighbor as themselves, Leviticus 19:18, contains another command just a few verses later.

When an alien resides with you in your land, you shall not oppress the alien. The alien who resides with you shall be to you as the citizen among you; you shall love the alien as yourself, for you were aliens in the land of Egypt: I am the Lord your God. (Lev. 19:33–34)

The Torah says that foreigners as well as neighbors are people we should love as ourselves. This is nothing new to the lawyer or Jesus's listeners. They've merely forgotten.

During a particularly vicious campaign season, when anti-immigrant rhetoric had grown heated, I changed the words of our church sign to read, "You shall love the alien as yourself." I received an angry phone message several days later from a woman who insisted that I was misquoting the

Bible and that nowhere in the scriptures were we commanded to love illegal aliens. While she may have been wrong about the scripture, she was right in that she understood the offense it was meant to cause. If we are to love our neighbors as ourselves, and aliens as ourselves, then we should love *everybody* as ourselves.

To understand the impact of this parable, it helps to shuffle the identity of the actors. We have been trained to imagine that this parable is an allegory, in which the Samaritan is like Jesus, who saves the poor sinner waylaid by life, and the church is like the innkeeper, who is charged to take care of the wounded until Jesus's return.

Instead of imagining the characters this way, some theologians have suggested a different angle. Susan Bond suggests that instead of calling this the Parable of the Good Samaritan, we should call it the Parable of the Man Who Fell among Thieves. In this interpretation, the wounded man, stripped naked and close to death, is Jesus on the cross, stretched between two thieves. Other elements of the story support this reading. The Samaritan, like Joseph of Arimathea, bandages the wounded Jesus. He places him on a donkey, like the one Jesus rode into Jerusalem. He takes him to an inn, like the one in which Jesus was born. The question for the listeners then becomes, "Who will recognize Jesus?" The story indicates it's not the people we expect. We religious people who claim to know Jesus often fail to recognize him:

> In the name of Jesus Christ, we can be downright un-neighborly. We run away from trouble and take care of ourselves. We escape with ski trips for the youth and Jazzercise for Jesus in the church basement. …Like Pilate at the crucifixion, we wash our hands of the whole affair. Or, like the Disciples, we stand at a safe distance and watch the crucifixion. We join in the betrayal. Our silence is approval.[76]

I opened this chapter with a story about a woman telling a reimagined parable of the Good Samaritan, because if Jesus told this parable to a

---

76   L. Susan Bond, "The Parable of the Man Who Fell among Thieves," *Biblical Preaching Journal*.

church in my own town, he would need to substitute some other religious in-groups for the passersby: Methodists, Presbyterians, Baptists, Lutherans. Whatever the case, the listeners in the congregation would expect their group representative, the hero, to show up in the last act. Instead, he would probably make the hero a Muslim, or an atheist, or a Mormon. Jesus would choose not one of our own group, but a member of a group we hate. He wouldn't let up, either. The antihero goes the extra mile, not only saving the wounded man's life, but treating him to extravagant hospitality.

It could be anyone from any group that our group hates: Republicans, Democrats, libertarians, agnostics, atheists, Mormons, gays, lesbians, evangelicals, militarists, environmentalists, labor unions, lawyers, communists, capitalists, immigrants, or nationalists. The principle of divine impartiality means that anyone we hate is a potential neighbor. The one who ultimately recognizes Jesus is the one who disregards social barriers, who throws in his lot with the forgotten, the wounded, or the crucified.

Just like Paul does in his letter to the Romans, Jesus demolishes even claims of religious exclusivity. If a Samaritan or a Gentile can do the will of God—can, in effect, recognize Jesus as the image of God in a person in need—then the doors of God's kingdom are blown wide open. If I admit that anyone can be my neighbor, and that anyone is capable of doing God's will and recognizing Jesus, then I admit that God commands me to love everyone, including my supposed enemies—even people of other religious persuasions.

Love Like You've Nothing to Lose

The most radical example of God's impartial love is the command to love our enemies. Jesus delivers this message in the Sermon on the Mount, the first chapter of which encourages his followers to hold to a high ethical principle—even higher than the Pharisees: "For I tell you, unless your righteousness exceeds that of the scribes and Pharisees, you will never enter the kingdom of heaven" (Matt. 5:20). He goes on to give concrete examples: resisting anger, lust, and oath-making. Finally he comes to how this new community should relate to evildoers:

You have heard that it was said, "An eye for an eye and a tooth for a tooth." But I say to you, Do not resist an evildoer. But if anyone strikes you on the right cheek, turn the other also; and if anyone wants to sue you and take your coat, give your cloak as well; and if anyone forces you to go one mile, go also the second mile. Give to everyone who begs from you, and do not refuse anyone who wants to borrow from you.

You have heard that it was said, "You shall love your neighbor and hate your enemy." But I say to you, Love your enemies and pray for those who persecute you, so that you may be children of your Father in heaven; for he makes his sun rise on the evil and on the good, and sends rain on the righteous and on the unrighteous. For if you love those who love you, what reward do you have? Do not even the tax-collectors do the same? And if you greet only your brothers and sisters, what more are you doing than others? Do not even the Gentiles do the same? Be perfect, therefore, as your heavenly Father is perfect. (Matt. 5:38–48)

Jesus's followers are to emulate God's impartial love, as children emulate the characteristics of their father, "for he makes his sun rise on the evil and the good, and sends rain on the righteous and on the unrighteous." Many biblical writers assumed that disaster was God's punishment, and prosperity was God's blessing. Jesus argues that God bestows gifts impartially. Sun and rain fall on everyone, both the wicked and the good. Holding his followers to a different standard, he points out, "If you love those who love you, what reward do you have? Do not even the tax collectors do the same?" When I hear these words I think of a funeral I was called on to do for an elderly woman I didn't know. I remember asking the family details about her life, so that I would have something to say during the service. She hadn't participated in the life of the church in decades, and as far as I could tell spent the last years of her life watching television and going to the beauty parlor for gossip. I fumbled around asking her family about hobbies, interests, passions, memorable holidays, anything that would help me get a handle on the character of the person whose life we were going to remember and celebrate. The family couldn't think of much to say. "You never had to wonder where you stood with her," her children said. "She told it like she saw it." I've learned over time that this is code language for "She was mean." One daughter confirmed my suspicion when she said, "If you messed with her family—watch out!"

I tried to ask, as delicately and nonjudgmentally as possible, what evidence did her family have that she had a relationship with Jesus? What did her faith mean to her? "She got saved when she was twelve, if that's what you mean." Yes, and how did you see her live that out? "Well, she loved her family."

For most people in the world, that's enough. But not for Jesus. "If you love those who love you, what reward do you have? If you greet only your brothers and sisters, what more are you doing than anyone else?" We talk about love of our children or our mothers as though that was some special virtue. The same could be said for Attila the Hun! Almost all people love their children and promote the interest of their own families above all others. Jesus says there is no extraordinary virtue in such things. Even tax collectors love their children and mothers. Loving your enemies, on the other hand, is something laudable. To love the wicked as well as the good means you love perfectly, even as God loves (Matt. 5:48).

In fact, love of family can become an obstacle to love of enemies. Perhaps this is why Jesus says in Matthew, "Whoever loves father or mother more than me is not worthy of me; and whoever loves son or daughter more than me is not worthy of me" (Matt. 10:37). In Luke, Jesus uses even stronger language: "Whoever comes to me and does not hate father and mother, wife and children, brothers and sisters, yes, and even life itself, cannot be my disciple" (Luke 14:26).[77]

We typically love the people in our group more and root for our causes against others because we believe in a world in which there are scarce resources. We keep our love small because we feel that loving big means

---

77 "Hate" is clearly a hyperbole. If Jesus had really meant "hate," he couldn't have reprimanded the Pharisees for not taking care of their aging parents (Matt. 15:4–5).

that our group or family will lose. This is why the modern nation of Israel continues to build settlements in Palestinian territory, and why anti-immigrant groups promote English-only language policies, and people in suburbs resist funding public transportation for fear that the urban poor will travel into their neighborhoods. We mark out our territories, build our gated communities, and invest in our own security because we believe that the sun and rain are scarce resources to be procured for our own group at the expense of others. And even if *we* don't believe that, there's danger for us if *they* do.

The ethic of impartial love that Jesus talks about is the ultimate expression of an ever-widening vision that begins in the Hebrew Bible and continues through his own ministry. It finds its practical expression in the early church, where all people are invited to the church regardless of their gender, economic status, age, or ethnicity. It is not an easy task that faces this new community. They must constantly struggle with how to live out this ideal. But the church is still a slice of the kingdom, a place where God's reign and impartial love are becoming real in a broken world. For the church, loving like Jesus means loving those outside the church *more* than the people inside the church. Jesus uses parables to make the same point: God goes after the one lost sheep, leaving behind the ninety-nine (Matt. 18:12). God spends all day looking for a single coin (Luke 15:8).

The Partiality of Jesus

The picture of the impartiality of Jesus wouldn't be complete without acknowledging times when he was obviously partial. Jesus was still very much a man of his culture. He himself was not entirely comfortable with Gentiles.

In Mark's gospel, just after declaring all foods clean and giving the Gentiles of Mark's church a handy slogan to use in debates with Pharisees, Jesus takes a retreat to the region of Tyre. A woman whose daughter is possessed by demons begs Jesus to cast them out of her. Mark tells us that she is the most Gentile of the Gentiles, a "Syrophoenician" woman.

Rather than respond with love and kindness like the Jesus we learn about in church, Jesus responds with a cutting remark. "Let the children be fed first, for it is not fair to take the children's food and throw it to the dogs" (Mark 7:27).

In our culture, "dog" is not particularly offensive. We keep dogs as pets, and even claim that they are part of the family. Calling someone a dog can even be a term of endearment. In much of the rest of the world, "dog" is still an insult, as it was in American and European culture in previous centuries. Calling someone a dog or a cur two hundred years ago could earn you a duel with someone whose honor you had besmirched.

We retain some of the old scandal in our own language, though we go through a roundabout way of evoking it. While "dog" has lost its offensiveness, "bitch" still retains some of its shock value. So, in order to call a man a dog, we call him a "son of a bitch"—which is simply a dog. Like most insults aimed at others in our culture, it takes the inclusion of someone's mother to make it *really* offensive.

So, when Jesus levels this oblique insult at the woman, she understands his meaning perfectly well. He has just called her a bitch. This is not a flattering picture of Jesus, and preachers and theologians have done all kinds of acrobatics to explain it in a way that will make us more comfortable. Maybe Jesus is just testing the woman, seeing how far she is willing to go. Maybe he doesn't mean it in a way as insulting as it seems.

Matthew adds a few details to the story to make it slightly less offensive. In his version, Jesus explains, "I was sent only to the lost sheep of the house of Israel" (Matt. 15:24). His ignoring the woman has nothing to do with prejudice, Matthew implies, but with him sticking to his mission. Earlier, when he commissions disciples to spread his message, he tells them, "Go nowhere among the Gentiles, and enter no town of the Samaritans, but go rather to the lost sheep of the house of Israel" (Matt. 10:5–6).

Yet it is only when she puts herself in a subordinate place to the children if Israel that Jesus relents. "Yet even the dogs eat the crumbs that fall from their masters' table," she says. Mark's Jesus approves of her subordinate status: "For saying that, you may go—the demon has left your daughter" (Mark 7:29). Matthew's Jesus, on the other hand, is impressed with her faith: "Then Jesus answered her, 'Woman, great is your faith! Let it be done for you as you wish'" (Matt. 15:28). The Matthew version is the preferred reading for people who want to claim that Jesus is merely testing the woman. Mark's earlier harsh version sticks in our craw.

Some claim that this is a conversion experience for Jesus. It's at this point that Jesus is challenged to put his radical words about cleanliness into practice and live it out. In Mark's next chapter, he travels to the Decapolis and other Gentile territories. Perhaps this moment with the Syrophoenician woman makes him aware that his mission is to a larger world.

Luke, who wants to emphasize Jesus's inclusion of women and foreigners, omits the story of the woman entirely, and when Luke's Jesus sends out the twelve, he puts no restrictions on where they should go (Luke 9:1–6). When Luke's Jesus decides to begin his long journey to Jerusalem, he even proposes going through a Samaritan village (Luke 9:51–56). When the villagers refuse him, his disciples want him to rain down fiery death on them, the way Elijah called down fire upon troops from Samaria (2 Kings 1:10). Jesus, demonstrating the impartial love of God even for his enemies, refuses.

I believe the early church chose to tell the story of the Syrophoenician woman because it illustrates another aspect of the principle of God's impartiality. There was clearly a danger that Gentile converts could become arrogant about their inclusion in the family of God. Paul hints at this possibility in Romans. He explicitly addresses the Gentiles and explains why they should not be arrogant toward non-Christian Jews:

> If some of the branches were broken off, and you, a wild olive shoot, were grafted in their place to share the rich root of the olive tree, do not boast over the branches. If you do boast, remember that it is not you that support the root, but the root that supports you. You will say, "Branches were broken off so that I might be grafted in." That is true. They were broken off because of their unbelief, but you stand only through faith. So do not become proud, but stand in awe. For if God did not spare the natural branches, perhaps he will not spare you. Note then the kindness and the severity of God:

severity towards those who have fallen, but God's kindness towards you, provided you continue in his kindness; otherwise you also will be cut off. And even those of Israel, if they do not persist in unbelief, will be grafted in, for God has the power to graft them in again. For if you have been cut from what is by nature a wild olive tree and grafted, contrary to nature, into a cultivated olive tree, how much more will these natural branches be grafted back into their own olive tree. (Rom. 11:17–24)

Paul intends to keep the Gentile Christians humble. They have been "grafted on" to the family tree of Abraham, and become part of God's saving action through a gracious gift. Paul wants to make sure that as he demolishes one barrier of partiality, he does not erect another. Gentiles should be grateful, Paul argues, not arrogant.

The story of the Syrophoenician woman functions the same way. It reflects the subordinate position Gentiles should feel toward this Jewish messiah. We are aliens to Jesus's religion, the unchosen people whose salvation comes entirely from grace and not from privilege. Just as the centurion tells Jesus he is not worthy to have Jesus underneath his roof (Matt. 8:8), the woman acknowledges she has no claim on God's gift but receives whatever he offers as a beggar.

Unfortunately, Christian churches have not been as careful. Anti-Jewish rhetoric and misunderstanding the role of the Pharisees in the ministry of Jesus has led Christians to treat Judaism as an incomplete religion, and to use "Pharisee" as a synonym for "legalist." We have hypocritically labeled Judaism as hypocritical and exclusive. We Christians have forgotten the slogan that God shows no partiality between Jews and Christians, and we have failed to apply the principle of God's impartiality, or to teach the history of the idea in the Hebrew Bible and the New Testament.

Loving with God's impartial love is not simply about the presupposition that all human beings are created equal and loved equally by their creator. It is not an ethic of generic inclusivity. The principle that God shows no partiality is rooted in self-giving love and an attitude of humility. We do not earn our salvation, nor can we boast in anything except the generosity of God. Today's churches often struggle with how to relate to other religions in a pluralistic world. The love ethic of Jesus is clear: out-love them. And don't be arrogant about it.

Although Jesus invites me to a place at the table, I do not approach it as if entitled to it. Jesus shows me where I belong by example. He is a servant, washing others' feet. He tells me not to seek the best place, but the lowest. I am a dog, scarfing up the crumbs that fall from the table. In the words of the Prayer of Humble Access in the communion liturgy,

> We do not presume to come to this thy Table, O merciful Lord, trusting in our own righteousness, but in thy manifold and great mercies. We are not worthy so much as to gather up the crumbs under thy Table. But it is your nature always to have mercy. We are not worthy that you should receive us, but only say the word and we shall be healed.[78]

While the story of the Syrophoenician woman does not show Jesus in the most flattering light, the principle and history of God's impartial love still makes itself heard. Even the unchosen have access to Jesus's mercy. Even the dogs get fed.

The Way, the Truth, and the Life

Our churches have forgotten this humble attitude because we have forgotten the slogan "God shows no partiality." Christian exclusivists have claimed that salvation comes only through Jesus Christ without recognizing what *kind* of Christ we worship. To them, the slogan that "God shows no partiality" is a threat. It opens the door to universal salvation, to works-righteousness, and to a loss of our distinctive Christian witness. If anyone can get in the club, what's the point of proclaiming Christ at all? Didn't Jesus say, "I am the way, the truth, and the life" and "No one comes to the Father except through me" (John 14:6)?

John's Jesus does indeed say these words. He says them at his last meal with the disciples, and he says them in answer to a particular question. Thomas and Philip are worried about Jesus's talk of dying. Jesus says that he is

---

78   *The Book of Common Prayer* (New York: Oxford University Press, 1990).

going to prepare a place for them, and then he says, "You know the way to the place where I am going" (14:4). Thomas, bewildered, says, "Lord, we do not know where you are going. How can we know the way?" Listen to his question very closely: Jesus says they know the way, but *Thomas doesn't know that he knows*. This is the same Thomas who, after the resurrection, refuses to believe Christ is raised until he sees Jesus for himself. Jesus tells this Thomas that he knows the way *before* he believes.

When Jesus tells the story of the sheep and the goats in Matthew (25:32-46), the sheep, like Thomas, do not know that they have been serving Jesus while they have been feeding the hungry and visiting the sick and imprisoned. They are as shocked as anyone that Jesus declares them righteous. It is not necessarily that their good deeds earned them anything, but that somehow the law of liberty written on their hearts compelled them to love their neighbors as themselves. They didn't recognize the way, the truth, and the life, even though they were serving him the whole time.

It is also apparently quite possible to hear and grasp that "Jesus is Lord," and still fail at showing allegiance to what that Lordship means. Twice Jesus warns against this possibility in Matthew. The first warning happens in the Sermon on the Mount:

> Not everyone who says to me, "Lord, Lord," will enter the kingdom of heaven, but only one who does the will of my Father in heaven. On that day many will say to me, "Lord, Lord, did we not prophesy in your name, and cast out demons in your name, and do many deeds of power in your name?" Then I will declare to them, "I never knew you; go away from me, you evildoers." (Matt. 7:21–23)

Clearly, knowing that Jesus is Lord is not enough. If we call Jesus "Lord," something about his character should indicate how we should live. It's not just about doing miracles and being religious: it's about compassion for others. He makes it more explicit in his second warning, which also comes from the parable of the sheep and the goats. Here again, the goats very clearly call Jesus "Lord." They just fail to recognize that Jesus is a Lord who shows no partiality, and they are blind to his presence in the hungry, the aliens, and the imprisoned.

Though Jesus tells him he knows the way, Thomas can't recognize God's saving power in the world standing right in front of him. How many people in the world may know Jesus without knowing that they know the way? How many Samaritans are binding up Jesus's wounds, feeding people in homeless shelters, digging wells in parched villages, holding the hands of grieving parents who have lost children, holding addicts accountable, and advocating for immigrant rights without ever knowing that they are doing it for Jesus? How many Doubting-Thomas agnostics who have rejected an exclusivist Christianity are following Jesus without ever knowing they are serving him as Lord?

Jesus replies to Thomas, "I am the way, the truth, and the life. No one comes to the Father except through me." In this context, Jesus is not cutting people out of the kingdom. Jesus is making a statement that is consistent with all his other statements in the book of John. "No one can come to me unless drawn by the Father who sent me…everyone who has heard and learned from the Father comes to me" (John 6:44-45). In other words, all of those tax collectors, prostitutes, and Samaritans who make the religious leaders nervous, who crowd around Jesus because they see God working in him, are drawn to him by *the God of Israel*.

Meanwhile, the religious leaders who reject Jesus do so because they do not truly understand the character of God. They are blinded by the masks they have been wearing. Jesus could just as easily say the same thing to Christian exclusivists: "You don't recognize my activity among gays, among Muslims, among agnostics, because you don't truly understand the character of my Father." He says as much to the religious leaders who accuse him of blasphemy: "You know neither me nor my Father. If you knew me, you would know my Father also" (John 8:19). If you get God, you get Jesus. If you get Jesus, you get God. Each reflects the true character of the other. This is what scandalizes the religious leaders, and this is why they conspire to eliminate him.

There is a growing awareness in churches that there is a different way to think about salvation. A shift has happened in the last few decades. Popular Christian authors question the doctrine of a literal hell. They point out that salvation is not just about going to heaven after we die. Many Christians who have felt alienated by the growth of the political Christian right, by exclusivist theologies and intolerance of homosexuals, have heard in these progressive theologies a prophetic word from God. The salvation project God began thousands of years ago is not about recruiting more people to a belief system or a Christian institution. It is about God's activity in the world, and a Way of Life opened to any who see and hear it.

I began this book by saying that "God shows no partiality" was a slogan, not a doctrine, and that while it was an important part of the gospel, it was not the entire gospel. Whenever I teach or preach about this slogan, someone nearly always asks the question, "Well, then, what *is* the gospel?" They are after the *kerygma*, the core of the Good News, the thing that Christians are supposed to preach and believe. I think the reason the slogan "God shows no partiality" generates this question is that it is difficult for us to think of salvation without immediately wondering who is in and who is out. We fear that if God shows no partiality, that Jesus Christ will become less important. As one author writes:

> It will always be easier to preach divine impartiality and the universal offer of salvation apart from the particularity of Christ; and perhaps, in our own day, this is the special temptation of the church. Yet the witness of Acts and the whole New Testament points in another direction: "There is salvation in no one else, for there is no other name under heaven among men by which we must be saved" (Acts 4:12). The Christian paradox is that salvation for all has been made accessible through the death of one man. God has manifested his divine impartiality through Jesus the Messiah, a member of the house of Israel.[79]

I am extremely skeptical that preaching divine impartiality or universal salvation is "easier" than preaching Christian exclusivism. It should be empirically observable: simply count the number of churches proclaiming one or the other to determine which is "easier." I believe churches that proclaim the Lordship and sovereignty of an impartial Christ have a greater

---

79   Frank J. Matera, "Acts 10:34-43," *Interpretation* 41, no. 1 (1987), 66.

challenge, the same way that Paul found it a greater challenge to resist the religious exclusivists of his day. As Susan Bond writes:

> The church's vocation is to risk its own corporate identity and life, to risk institutional death, in pursuit of God's beyond-the-church future. We are not called to conquer the world for Christ or to make Christians out of non-Christians. To claim the Lordship of Christ is to set aside all human schemes of insider/outsider and to point toward a world that God desires.[80]

God's impartiality creates anxiety for Christians who wish to preserve what they understand as the traditional core content of the gospel, which is the unique character and divinity of Christ. My personal theology is that the unique character and divinity of Christ cannot be separated from the proclamation of the whole story, including his impartiality. Calling Jesus "Christ" and "Lord" only makes sense in a particular context. The message of salvation is, in part, that Jesus is *not* a Lord like other lords. His title is synonymous with the reversal of human ways of thinking about the world. God is not a God who demands that human beings fulfill a certain set of criteria before God will act, whether those criteria are circumcision, or food regulations, or saying the sinner's prayer, or membership in a church. If we say, "Jesus is Lord," the follow-up question should always be, "What kind of lord?" The early church had an answer: the kind of Lord who embodies the impartiality of God, who sees behind the mask, who will ultimately unmask all the actors and reveal the cosmic drama going on all around us. This is not merely about love triumphing *over* justice. This is about love made perfect *in* God's justice as people are unmasked and God loves them to completion.

The gospels were written with an agenda, to tell the story of an impartial Jesus who was the representative of an impartial God in a very partial world. The followers of Jesus were to live with a sense that God would eventually unmask the world, that secular sinners were no worse than religious hypocrites, and that the church should be a community that reflects God's impartiality. The humility with which the Gentile Christians received this message should be the same humility we express today.

---

80   Bond, "Acts 10:34-43."

CHAPTER 6:

THE GREAT UNMASKING

Nothing is covered up that will not be uncovered, and nothing secret
that will not become known.
Luke 12:1

It's a Wonderful Life

I'm dead. The last thing I remember from my life before is my family looking down at me and murmuring their good-byes, their eyes filled with tears
as I slipped away into the darkness. The next thing I know, I'm hearing my
name called, and when I open my eyes again I'm standing before the throne
of God. I know it's God because the Creator is wrapped in a thick cloud of
darkness and fire blazes from within. Above the cloud is a light so bright
that its intensity threatens to unmake me, but I've seen *Raiders of the Lost
Ark*; I know better than to look at the face of God. I have arrived at my own
personal judgment day. An angel who looks remarkably like the bailiff Bull
Shannon in *Night Court* steps forward. "David," he says, "you have been
called to give an account of the life your Creator gave you. Are you ready?"

"I guess so."

"Witnesses, are you ready?"

I turn and look behind me and see all of creation. My chest spasms. All
of the universe's sentient creatures are assembled, row upon row, fading
into eternity. Somehow I can pick out the faces of every one of my friends
and family: my grandfather, my younger sister, my high school English
teacher, my wife, and even great grandchildren that I do not yet know. I
see people I have taught and mentored who have looked up to me. I also
see my enemies: the boy who made my seventh grade year a living hell, a

woman who still bears a grudge for some of my pastoral decisions, and the lot owner who impounded my broken-down car in Georgia. There are also beings that represent the plants and animals whose lives I took thoughtlessly through wasteful living, children whose water I polluted, and people in poverty I ignored.

"If you'll turn your attention to the screen."

I turn back toward my Judge as creation goes dark. An enormous movie screen descends from the sky. A black-and-white countdown leader flashes "5, 4, 3, 2…"

"Wait, what's happening?" I ask.

"We're going to watch a movie of your life," the angel explains.

"What, my whole life?"

The angel smiles and nods excitedly. "Exactly," he says, "complete with director's commentary and multitrack audio insight into your thoughts and feelings. We can pause, rewind, and watch from multiple angles. We'll hear every murmured insult, uncharitable thought, and duplicitous motivation that were hidden to regular viewers. Using quantum screen-within-a-screen technology, we'll even be able to see the consequences of your actions that you never witnessed and the lives of all the beings you impacted."

If I still have blood in the afterlife, it drains from my face. "Is everyone going to see this?" I ask.

Still smiling, the angel bubbles with enthusiasm. "Oh, absolutely! We can spend an infinite amount of time on each person, and we have this particular dimension of eternity to spend entirely on you. Have some popcorn."

I turn and glance behind me at the billions of eyes reflecting the images on screen in the darkened theater. Their expressions are unreadable. I do not know whose gaze I fear the most: my enemies' or my friends'. And then, remembering the Judge on the throne, I am embarrassed that I am more concerned about their approval than God's own.

And there is my life in front of me, in high-definition and surround-sound: disastrous junior high dances, derisive laughter and bullying I received and doled out, words spoken in anger and endless regret afterward, lustful actions sweet in the moment but bitter in retrospect, apathy in the face of injustice, that time we convinced a younger boy that our urine was lemonade, etc., etc., etc. Things I never wanted anyone to find out. Everything I wanted to forget. The shame makes my face burn.

But I also see things I had forgotten. A smile that lifted someone's day. An anonymous gift of generosity. Time spent with someone who felt lonely. Good advice given to a friend, and a listening ear when words failed. A letter written to my legislator or a courageous sermon preached that addressed social injustice. Good deeds which I was willing to write off as no more valuable than filthy rags are noticed, celebrated, and multiplied by grace. I hear applause during scenes that seem totally inappropriate. "Wait," I say, "but I wasn't trying to be a hero. I wasn't doing anything special."

"You think that matters?" asks the angel.

There are bonus scenes and special features at the end of the movie: interviews with people whose lives I touched, people I love and people I do not. A woman for whom I harbored a secret contempt says, "He never said an unkind word to me. He always took time to listen." A man I respect deeply as an authority in his field says, "He taught me so much." Their praise is embarrassing. I feel both like George Bailey in the movie *It's a Wonderful Life* and Ebenezer Scrooge in *A Christmas Carol.* I see my own life as a painfully beautiful gift. My face is wet with tears, and I hear myself repeating, "I never knew. I just never knew."

At the end of the movie, when the lights come up, after the cinematic light of truth in the darkened theater has burned away the parts of me that were fake and revealed me for who I truly am, I stand naked before my Creator and, trembling, finally have the courage to look into those eyes. I no longer care about the opinion of the rest of creation, yet at the same time I am grateful for all of it. And in some other eternity, I take my place in the audience and watch the lives of my friends—there are no enemies any more—with new vision. Now that I know intimately my own failures and the grace I do not deserve, I cannot look at anyone the same way. Though the injustices others commit and the pain they inflict on themselves and others are no less real or evil, I have to look at them more kindly. Since I have been exposed before all creation as a fraud and a hypocrite, but still received grace, how could I condemn others?

The End of All Things

In some ways, this event is similar to what Fredrick Nietzsche called "eternal recurrence." He poses this question: If you knew you would have to relive your life exactly the way you live it now, would it be hell or would it be heaven?[81] Or would it be both? To Nietzsche's own atheistic and lonely fantasy I've merely added God and the presence of a great cloud of witnesses.

Of course, I do not think this is what really happens when we die, but I do think it's a useful image for exploring the concept of God's judgment and the end of the age. Biblical authors often talk about God's reign as a time when light will shine in dark places and secret things will be exposed. The author of Psalm 90:8 talks about having our sins set before the light of God's countenance. "There is nothing hidden, except to be disclosed; nor is anything secret, except to come to light," Jesus says in Mark 4:22. He warns his disciples not to become religious hypocrites themselves:

Beware of the yeast of the Pharisees, that is, their hypocrisy. Nothing is covered up that will not be uncovered, and nothing secret that will not become known. Therefore whatever you have said in the dark will be heard in the light, and what you have whispered behind closed doors will be proclaimed from the housetops. (Luke 12:1–3)

While most Biblical authors speak of it in the future tense, as a kingdom or a judgment that has not yet come, others speak of it as a present reality. According to John's gospel, it is the very presence of Jesus that illuminates the world and separates good from evil and truth from lies:

And this is the judgment, that the light has come into the world, and people loved darkness rather than light because their deeds were evil. For all who do evil hate the light and do not come to the light, so that their deeds may not be exposed. But those who do what is true come to the light, so that it may be clearly seen that their deeds have been done in God. (John 3:19–21)

---

81   Friedrich Nietzsche, *The Gay Science*, 341.

Somehow the end of the age, the judgment of God, and the presence of Jesus are all the same thing and have the same effect. The intense light of God's gaze exposes everything for what it is.

At Jesus's birth, Simeon prophesies that Jesus "is destined for the falling and the rising of many in Israel, and to be a sign that will be opposed so that the inner thoughts of many will be revealed" (Luke 2:34-35). Jesus turns the social order upside-down. The early church looked forward to the day that Jesus would return and rule the world. He would be the judge who would separate the nations into sheep and goats:

> Then the king will say to those at his right hand, "Come, you that are blessed by my Father, inherit the kingdom prepared for you from the foundation of the world; for I was hungry and you gave me food, I was thirsty and you gave me something to drink, I was a stranger and you welcomed me, I was naked and you gave me clothing, I was sick and you took care of me, I was in prison and you visited me." Then the righteous will answer him, "Lord, when was it that we saw you hungry and gave you food, or thirsty and gave you something to drink? And when was it that we saw you a stranger and welcomed you, or naked and gave you clothing? And when was it that we saw you sick or in prison and visited you?" And the king will answer them, "Truly I tell you, just as you did it to one of the least of these who are members of my family, you did it to me." (Matt. 25:34–40)

Just as in the story I told in the beginning of the chapter, there would be a great unmasking. Though in this case it would not be the people who were unmasked, but Jesus himself, who had been disguised as "the least of these." Once Jesus is revealed as already present in the world in the form of everyone who is hungry, sick, or imprisoned, the rest of humanity is unmasked as either sheep or goats. Those goats who had worn masks of righteousness and religiosity are revealed to be posers who cared nothing for Jesus, while those sheep who had figured themselves on the outside of the salvation story find that they've known Jesus all along. The author of Hebrews says that "the word of God is living and active, sharper than any two-edged sword, piercing until it divides soul from spirit, joints from marrow; it is able to judge the thoughts and intentions of the heart" (Heb. 4:12).

When the biblical authors talk about the judgment and wrath of God, they often talk about it as a purging or refining fire. These are the fires that, in the popular imagination of traditional religion, stoke the flames of hell.[82] But an alternative interpretation of these passages is that this fire is the refining love of God and that all God actually has to do to punish or reform us is to reveal us to ourselves. One of the words translated as "hell" in the New Testament was the name of Jerusalem's garbage dump, *Gehenna,* a place of fire, scavengers, and decay. In Brian McLaren's book about judgment and the afterlife, one of his characters explores the metaphor of hell being like a garbage dump:

> Don't all [these images] suggest waste, decay, regret, and sorrow? Isn't that what anyone would feel if he spent his whole life accumulating possessions or wealth or knowledge or power but missed out on life to the full in the kingdom of God? He would have wasted his life! He would have failed to become the glorious person he could have become and instead become something crabby and cramped and ingrown and dark and shabby and selfish. Wouldn't that make you weep and gnash your teeth?

> ...That's what judgment means: before the just judge, the truth comes out. Hypocrisy and fraud are uncovered, burned away. ... Everything that's worthless or fruitless will be exposed as worthless, and everything that's worthwhile and fruitful will be celebrated, rewarded, saved.[83]

---

82 In recent years, popular Christian authors like Rob Bell and Brian McLaren have openly questioned the doctrine of hell, and have suggested to evangelical audiences that perhaps God's salvation is about more than just going to heaven when we die. The gospel means abundant life here and now in this life. These are not new ideas. They have been around for ages. But I'm excited to see them gain traction among Christians who are looking for something deeper and wider than most churches have been offering them.
83 McLaren, *The Last Word and the Word after That,* 107.

There are a wide variety of theological opinions on biblical end times,[84] heaven and hell, and the judgment of God. Some Christians have very literal interpretations of such things. I remember one fundamentalist arguing, "The Bible doesn't say hell is a metaphor! It says in Revelation that hell is a lake of fire and it burns!"[85] My goal here is not to flesh out a complete theology of the afterlife or of the end of the age. I simply want to point out that unmasking, revealing, and shining the light of truth into the dark corners of our world is part of God's project for creation. While it may be terrifying to think of our identity as sinners, frauds, and hypocrites being exposed, most biblical authors seem to think of this as a *good* thing.

The kingdom of God means not only judgment but also hope. By revealing evil for what it is, we are freed from its shackles. Good things that have been buried under an avalanche of evil will be allowed to flourish. The writer of Ecclesiastes says that "God will bring every deed into judgment, including every secret thing, whether good or evil." When preaching to his disciples in the Sermon on the Mount, Jesus advises his followers to be more righteous than the Pharisees, but not for the purposes of receiving public praise. Whether his followers give, pray, or fast, they should do so "in secret," so that their Father who sees them in secret will reward them (Matt. 6:4, 6, 18).

Although the popular imagination focuses on the end of the world in movies and religious literature as fiery destruction or zombie apocalypse, the coming kingdom of God is a different kind of "end." The word "end" can also mean "goal," and so when we talk about the "end" of the age or of the world, we can talk about what God's goal is for all of creation. The end or the purpose of the world is not fiery death and destruction. The end of the world is healing and restoration, hope and liberation.

Hope and Liberation

When I told a fellow preacher about the thesis of this book, he was intrigued. I asked him to read an early draft and to give be an honest

---

84 Eschaton is the Greek word for the end times or the last things.
85 Actually, in Revelation 20:14, "hell" itself (Hades) is thrown into a lake of fire along with death, suggesting an end to hell.

critique. "I really like what you have to say," he said, "but my question is this: How do you prevent this idea from turning into a kind of generic, mushy inclusiveness?"

After my friend expressed his critique, I wondered out loud how "generic, mushy inclusiveness" would sound to someone who was gay who had watched as religious organizations and politicians looking to score points had tried to pass legislation forbidding him to adopt children, or teach in a classroom, or serve openly in the military. I wondered how it would sound to the interracial couple recently kicked out of their rural hometown church. To people who have historically experienced exclusion by religious people who declared them "profane or unclean," a little generic, mushy inclusion might be welcome.

At the same time, the critique is still a good one. As I said in chapter one, there is a difference between a slogan and a doctrine. Though the slogan "God shows no partiality" has theological underpinnings, it is not meant to be doctrine, and it only makes sense when we hold it up in opposition to the extreme partiality and injustice of humanity.

The idea that God shows no partiality was a revelation to Peter in Acts 10:34. It was a basic truth in which Paul believed. It shaped the practices of the early church. But it was not a "blind" impartiality. It was rooted in the idea that in spite of the tangled webs we weave out of coercive language, social control, and unjust systems, there actually is a fundamental truth that Jesus exposes. If God shows no partiality in judging the slaveholder and the slave, it is not because the institution of slavery is irrelevant. God will judge slave, slaveholder, and the institution of slavery according to God's own impartiality.[86] If God shows no partiality in inviting uncircumcised Gentiles to share a common table with Jewish Christians, it is not because twelve hundred years of religious practice and nationalist pride has evaporated. If we proclaim salvation for the world for all people, it is not because we ignore the centrality of Christ in salvation history, but because we affirm it. The Lord we proclaim is a Lord who shows no partiality.

---

86   Paul's letter to Philemon expresses this very idea. When he sends Onesimus back to his owner, Philemon, he suggests that Philemon should willingly bring him back into his household, "no longer as a slave, but as a beloved brother" (Philemon 16)

Just as any other passage or saying from the Bible, "God shows no partiality" could be abused. I have witnessed more than one situation in which child predators were allowed to continue attending worship services with their victims because churches were reluctant to seem ungracious or judgmental toward molesters "before all the facts were in." This is not impartiality. It is irresponsibility. We are not allowed to recuse ourselves of making human judgments, and in fact the desire to do so, to be above reproach, is itself a symptom of sin. We allow injustices to continue in the name of fairness rather than get our hands dirty by making tough decisions about ethics and policy. "God shows no partiality" could be used as just such a mask. People who are bullies or who support bullying systems of power often pretend to be victims and plead for fairness even as they continue to hurt others.

Theologian Langdon Gilkey spent nearly three years between 1943 and 1945 in an internment camp in China under Japanese occupation. In his book *Shantung Compound*, he detailed the ways the 1,450 prisoners who were professors, businessmen, lawyers, clergy, and families from many different countries tried to organize their lives. One Christmas, the American Red Cross delivered 1,550 care parcels to the camp. The parcels contained food that the prisoners desperately needed. The Japanese authorities originally figured they would distribute one parcel to every prisoner and give the two hundred Americans an extra half-parcel each since the parcels came from America. But a small party of American prisoners insisted that, since the parcels were from the *American* Red Cross and were American property, every American should get *seven*. This small but powerful minority created gridlock in the camp. Fights erupted along national lines among people who had previously been friends. The Japanese authorities refused to distribute the parcels until some kind of compromise was worked out.

Gilkey describes how he visited some of his fellow Americans and tried to talk them into compromising. One simply said, "I'm American, and these sandwiches are mine. I'm going to see I get every one that's coming to me." A lawyer took a more intellectual approach. He insisted it wasn't his own self-interest that led him to oppose distributing the parcels to the other prisoners:

I'm not worried about the parcels—about how many I or the other Americans may get. With me it's the principle that counts. We've got to make sure in this hellhole, whatever price we have to pay in popularity, that the rights of American property are preserved and respected. We've got to be faithful executors of the American Red Cross donors who sent these here for our use.[87]

The missionary, though, was the one who invoked a high-minded religious reason for his greed. "There is no virtue in being forced to share. We Americans should be given the parcels, all right. Then each of us should be left to exercise his own moral judgment in deciding what to do with them. We will share, but not on order from the enemy, for then it would not be moral."[88]

These seven Americans held up the distribution of food to the entire camp even though *most* of their fellow countrymen seemed to agree it was wrong. Yet when it came down to a vote, the Americans on the fence sided with the seven. The thin veneer of legal and moral righteousness soothed their consciences enough to allow their real motivation, their greed, to hold sway.

The story ends with bitter poetic justice. When the American contingent made it clear to the Japanese authorities that they would not allow the food to be distributed among anyone other than the Americans, the guards accepted their judgment. Two hundred parcels were distributed among the two hundred Americans. The remaining 1,350 were sent to another camp.

In our society, these same forces are at play. People co-opt religious and legal language to mask their motivations. They use hatred and fear to encourage people to serve their own short-sighted interests. Small minorities of the rich and powerful buy influence among legislators, and in the process we hurt ourselves, others, and the planet. We live in a world in which such coalitions of the rich and powerful are even granted legal "personhood" by law. We call them "corporations" (which literally means "bod-

---

87   Langdon Gilkey, *Shantung Compound* (Harper: HarperSanFrancisco, 1966), 108.
88   Gilkey, *Shantung Compound*, 109.

ies") and they, too, wear a *prosopon,* a mask of legitimacy.[89] These powers and principalities, the petty tyrant gods of this world, resist the coming kingdom of God because they fear being unmasked and revealed for what they are. Yet when it comes time to hold these corporate "persons" responsible for their actions, to put them on trial for negligent pollution of our planet, for land-grabbing politics in developing countries that displace subsistence farmers and people in poverty, for fraud, insider trading, and practices that wreck the global economy, their leaders abandon the language of personhood and talk about mysterious abstract market forces as if they were irresistible and inevitable laws like gravity or entropy. Suddenly these persons become ghosts, without moral agency, social responsibility, or legal accountability, all of which are part of what it means to be a real human person.

To claim allegiance to an impartial Lord, then, is to prophesy that the days of these powers and principalities are numbered. Something like the judgment-movie scene I described earlier will play out with regard not only to individuals, but to the systems of dominion and control that keep people from flourishing and becoming the creatures God created them to be. Jesus is the judge of *nations*, not just individuals. In the meantime, by following Jesus and proclaiming the rule of our impartial Lord, we resist the people and institutions that enslave and hurt human beings and their world.

The claim that God shows no partiality is not a retreat into moral relativism. It is a recognition that morality and law, which claim to be impartial, are often covers for the forces of darkness. God is the only one who is capable of being completely impartial. We who proclaim God's reign still have to live in the real world and navigate the tricky path between comforting the afflicted and afflicting the comfortable.

One of the strengths of the Christian faith is that it contains a curious self-critical tendency that (ideally) leads people to be reflective about their moral judgments. We are all simultaneously sinners and saints, Martin Luther said, and the recognition of that fact should make us circumspect

---

89   Ironically, the word "person" is from the Latin word that also means "mask."

about our religious claims. When we come into a Christian community, it should be with the recognition that everyone there is a sinner. By acknowledging and confessing our sin to each other, we are freed from the burden of having to wear a mask anymore.

One of my favorite worship services of the year is Ash Wednesday. It marks the beginning of Lent, a season of reflection and repentance. Forty days before Easter, people arrive at church early in the morning or in the evening, and the pastor imposes ashes on their foreheads in the sign of the cross, saying "Remember you are dust, and to dust you will return," or "Repent, and believe the gospel." Afterward, we look at each other, dark smudges on our foreheads, and we realize that everyone around us is a sinner saved by grace. The junkie and the banking executive both bear the sign of ashes on their face, their *prosopon*, a reminder that, in the end, they will both turn into dirt. Judgment and mercy, wrath and love are marked on the mask they present to the world.

Ideally, this idea transforms how I interact with everyone. It is a bit like shaking hands and introducing yourself by saying, "Hi, I'm a greedy, lustful, intolerant, racist, addicted, self-centered bastard. And you are?" If nothing else, it would change the tenor of our conversations. Like members of Alcoholics Anonymous, we would speak with an understanding that everyone in the room is as screwed up as we are. We would recognize that we have a tendency to lie to ourselves or each other. Even when we try our hardest, we cannot be impartial. We need the insight of others to call us to task.

Swords into Plowshares

People do use the Bible as a weapon. They climb up on high pulpits and drop Bibles on peoples' heads, clobbering people who disagree with them about homosexuality, or the ordination of women, or social justice for the poor. Some Christians actually refer to their Bible as their "sword," with which they will wage a spiritual war. It is a misuse of the Bible. If we sit down and read it, struggle with it, grapple with it, and let it change us, we cannot use it as a weapon. The Word of God may be sharper than any two-edged sword, but it should not be used as the sword of oppression. It is the sword of truth which pierces our own souls and challenges us to live authentic lives before a holy God.

What I have found in teaching the Bible in both the academy and the church is that the people who believe in the Bible most literally are often the least literate about it. They may have memorized favorite scriptures that support their own opinions, but they do not often read the minor prophets, and they have no idea what the Babylonian Exile was. They are essentially writing their own Bibles, and the versions they come up with have little to do with the actual history and social movements that created the religion of ancient Israel or that gave birth to the church. When I press literalists about their interpretation of scripture, asking them to explain contradictions or inconsistencies in their favorite texts, they invariably will complain that I'm reading *too* literally, that I'm nitpicking or reading too closely.

My gripe with progressive Christians, on the other hand, is that they have often ceded the Bible and Christian history to Christian fundamentalists and literalists. They have been on the defensive, relying on generalizations and failing to engage believers with powerful biblical rhetoric. Having been wounded one too many times by scripture-wielding exclusivists, perhaps they are reluctant to engage scripture on social issues at all.

But the history of the early church and God's activity among us is a powerful witness. In writing this book, I have hoped to challenge progressive Christians to actively engage the Bible—not with proof-texts and scriptures cherry-picked to support a given position, but with thoughtful exploration using the best scholarship available.

Doing so will inevitably lead to resistance. There are plenty of people who believe they own the Bible, and that it is their right to clobber people with it. Other people have echoed my son's words to me: "You wicked, wicked man! You can't take God's word away from me!" Sometimes these are unwinnable battles, and engaging them is a waste of time. In one well-known parable, Jesus describes hearers of the gospel as different kinds of soil (Mark 4:1–9) and the seed planted in them faces different obstacles to its growth. The germinating seed may be eaten, crushed, baked, or strangled. We can give all kinds of reasons that people might resist the gospel:

learned helplessness, demonic or political possession, selfishness and materialism, or social pressure. Yet the slogan I have been promoting in this book is one the world needs to hear. By making it better known, we will transform the Bible from a sword into a plow. Perhaps instead of waging a war against sword-wielding Christians who will not be convinced, we can dig furrows and plant new seeds among those who are receptive to the Good News. At the end of the parable, after all, there is a harvest—thirty-, sixty-, and a hundredfold.

Sharing the News

If you, dear reader, are someone who does believe that God shows no partiality, if you look forward to the day that the powers and principalities are unmasked, there are some practical things you can do to turn the rhetorical sword the Bible has become into a plowshare that helps bring new life. Here are some practical steps.

First, Christians who believe in the salvation of the world should delve deeply into scripture. It is essential to study the Bible closely, to listen thoughtfully to what the authors say and do not say. Do not accept the pious reflections of preachers or the footnotes of popular study Bibles as the word of God. Read multiple translations, and be open to diverse interpretations. Ask how a given scripture might sound different to a white man, a black woman, or a religious or political prisoner. Ask what situations the authors faced and what voices they were arguing against. Study the Bible with people who have diverse theological opinions so you can hear with new ears. Be willing to read against the grain.

Second, if you want to resist those who use the Bible as a weapon, you must exceed them in good works. Jesus's Sermon on the Mount is essentially a long discourse on how the new community should not only reject the principles of the Christian Pharisee faction, but distinguish themselves in practice. Their righteousness "must exceed that of the Pharisees" (Matt. 5:20). If progressive Christians want to be taken seriously by the world, they must out-pray, out-give, out-do, and out-sacrifice their fundamentalist siblings. They must live lives of exceptional moral conduct and generosity. If they do not, they will face two consequences: they will lose their social persuasiveness and they will become hypocrites themselves. This exceptional moral conduct is not just a matter of surface religiosity. It is about a transformation that happens to the soul (Matt. 5:44).

Third, you must spread the good news. The word "evangel" literally means "good message." Fundamentalists tend to be evangelical because they believe they are saving people from hell in the afterlife. Progressive Christians are trying to save people from hell in this life, but they often fail to be evangelical even though I believe their good news is often more compelling and more exciting. I believe the news is just as good now as it was in the first century. If we do as Jesus instructed and spread this good news to all the earth, then burgeoning Christian movements in developing countries will not criminalize homosexuality or silence the voices of women. People in America will not be able to reject Christianity out-of-hand as intolerant and irrational—but only if this message spreads.

"God shows no partiality" is a slogan, theological principle, and core value that shows up too often in the writings of the New Testament to be a coincidence. It was a saying that shaped the activity of the early church, and if we go back and reread the letters and gospels with this slogan in mind, we can see how those early church conflicts shaped the writing of the scriptures. The conflicts that challenged the early church regarding inclusion and exclusion, or social policies and group politics, are the same ones that challenge us today, the same ones we have been struggling with through two thousand years of church history.

I am not naive enough to think that simply reclaiming this biblical slogan will solve our churches' struggles with social issues. It did not make the problems of the ancient church go away, and it will not make ours go away, either. But I am idealistic enough (and perhaps naive enough) to believe that it is possible to create a church in which Pharisees and pagans are welcome to the table of Christ, and where it is possible to disagree without being disrespectful. I am idealistic enough to believe that Christ's one body has muscles in it that pull in different directions, and that its fingers will get more work done if they have a thumb to oppose. It would be unfortunate if we were all fingers, or all thumbs!

I hope this slogan will become as ubiquitous as others plastered on billboards and bumper stickers around the country. I hope Christians will latch on to it and use it as the biblical basis for their struggle against racism, classism, homophobia, and elitism. And I hope others will be drawn to this Jesus Christ who embodied the life of a God who shows no partiality.

BIBLIOGRAPHY

"Sayings Gospels," in *The Complete Gospels*, edited by Robert J. Miller, 247–366. Santa Rosa, CA: Polebridge Press, 1994.

Bassler, Jouette M. *Divine Impartiality: Paul and a Theological Axiom*. Chico, CA: Scholars Press, 1982.

Boehm, Omri. "Child Sacrifice, Ethical Responsibility and the Existence of the People of Israel." *Vetus Testamentum* 54, no. 2 (2004): 145–56.

The Book of Common Prayer. New York: Oxford University Press, 1990.

Bond, L. Susan. "Acts 10:34-43." *Interpretation* 56, no. 1 (2002): 80–83.

———. "The Parable of the Man Who Fell among Thieves."*Biblical Preaching Journal*.

Buttrick, David. *Speaking Parables*. Louisville, KY: John Knox, 2000.

Campbell, Douglas. *The Deliverance of God: An Apocalyptic Rereading of Justification in Paul*. Grand Rapids, MI: Eerdmans, 2009.

Cohick, Lynn H. *Women in the World of the Earliest Christians: Illuminating Ancient Ways of Life*. Grand Rapids, MI: Baker Academic, 2009.

Crossan, John Dominic. *The Historical Jesus: The Life of a Mediterranean Jewish Peasant*. San Francisco: Harper, 1991.

———. *In Search of Paul: How Jesus's Apostle Opposed Rome's Empire with God's Kingdom*. San Francisco: HarperSanFrancisco, 2004.

Douglas, Mary. "Justice as the Cornerstone: An Interpretation of Leviticus 18–20." *Interpretation* 53, no. 4 (1999): 341–50.

Elliott, Neil. *Liberating Paul: The Justice of God & the Politics of the Apostle*. Minneapolis, MN: Fortress, 1994.

Gilkey, Langdon. *Shantung Compound*. San Francisco: HarperSanFrancisco, 1966.

Goldingay, John. "The Significance of Circumcision." *Journal for the Study of the Old Testament* 88 (2000): 3–18.

Gundry-Volf, Judith M. "The Least and the Greatest," in *The Child in Christian Thought*, edited by Marcia J. Bunge, 29–60. Grand Rapids, MI: Eerdmans, 2001.

Hauerwas, Stanley. "The August Partiality of God's Love." *Reformed Journal* 39, no. 5 (1989): 10–12.

Hester, J. David. "Eunuchs and the Postgender Jesus: Matthew 19:12 and Transgressive Sexualities." *Journal for the Study of the New Testament* 28, no. 1 (2005): 13–40.

Hornsby, Teresa. *Sex Texts from the Bible*. Woodstock, NY: SkyLight Paths.

Krentz, Edgar. "Egalitarian Church of Matthew." *Currents in Theology and Mission* 4, no. 6 (1977): 333–41.

Lipschutz, Marion and Rose Rosenblatt. *The Education of Shelby Knox*. Incite Pictures, 2005.

Maccoby, Hyam. *Jesus the Pharisee*. London: SCM Press, 2000.

———. *Revolution in Judaea: Jesus and the Jewish Resistance*. New York: Taplinger, 1981.

Martin, Troy W. "Paul's Argument from Nature for the Veil in 1 Corinthians 11:13–15: A Testicle Instead of a Head Covering." *Journal of Biblical Literature* 123, no. 1 (2004): 75–84.

Matera, Frank J. "Acts 10:34–43." *Interpretation* 41, no. 1 (1987): 62–66.

McLaren, Brian. *The Last Word and the Word after That: A Tale of Faith, Doubt, and a New Kind of Christianity*. San Francisco: Jossey-Bass, 2005.

NPR. "Pilgrims Trace Women's Role in Early Church." April 16, 2006. Radio.

Pope, Stephen J. "Proper and Improper Partiality and the Preferential Option for the Poor." *Theological Studies* 54, no. 2 (1993): 242–71.

Powell, Mark Allan. *Fortress Introduction to the Gospels*. Minneapolis. MN: Fortress, 1998.

Sasson, Jack M. "Circumcision in the Ancient near East." *Journal of Biblical Literature* 85, no. 4 (1966): 473–76.

Scurlock, Jo Ann. "One Hundred Sixty-Seven BCE: Hellenism or Reform?" *Journal for the Study of Judaism in the Persian, Hellenistic and Roman Period* 31, no. 2 (2000): 125–61.

Siker, Jeffrey S. "How to Decide? Homosexual Christians, the Bible, and Gentile Inclusion as Model for Contemporary Debate over Gays and Lesbians." *Theology Today* 51, no. 2 (1994): 219–34. Spencer, Tim. *Cigareets, Whusky & Wild Women*. BMI, 1946.

The United Methodist Hymnal. Nashville, TN: The United Methodist Publishing House, 1989.

Volf, Miroslav. *Exclusion and Embrace*. Nashville, TN: Abingdon, 1996.

Wesley, John. "Sermon 116: Causes of the Inefficacy of Christianity." *Global Ministries*, 2011. http://new.gbgm-umc.org/umhistory/wesley/sermons/116/.

Wiesenberg, Ernest. "Related Prohibitions: Swine Breeding and the Study of Greek." *Hebrew Union College Annual* 27 (1956): 213–33.

Wright, N. T. *What Saint Paul Really Said*. Cincinnati, OH: Eerdmans, 1997.

Wyatt, Nicolas. "Circumcision and Circumstance: Male Genital Mutilation in Ancient Israel and Ugarit." *Journal for the Study of the Old Testament* 33, no. 4 (2009): 405–31.

SCRIPTURE INDEX

ABOUT THE AUTHOR

Dave Barnhart is a pastor and ordained elder in the North Alabama Conference of the United Methodist Church. He earned his Ph.D. in homiletics and social ethics from Vanderbilt University in 2004, and his M.Div. from Candler School of Theology in 1997. He is the author of *What's in the Bible About Church?* (Abingdon, 2009). His sermons have appeared in the *Abingdon Preaching Annual*. He lives in Birmingham, Alabama with his wife and son.